MW01289462

THE BIBLE:
THE TRUTH
ABOUT PSYCHICS
&
SPIRITUAL GIFTS

KEVIN SCHOEPPEL

THE BIBLE:
THE TRUTH
ABOUT PSYCHICS
&
SPIRITUAL GIFTS

Printed and published in the United States of America

ISBN: 1484127668
ISBN-13: 978-1484127667

Stir up the gift of God, which is in thee. . .
for God hath not given us the spirit of fear;
but of power, and of love, and of a sound mind.
~ 2 Timothy 1:6-7 (KJV)

This book is dedicated to my wife, Stanna, and my son, Ryan. May God use your gifts for His glory.

ACKNOWLEDGEMENTS

My sole acknowledgement for the contents of this book is the
Spirit of the Lord:

In all thy ways acknowledge him, and he shall direct thy paths.
~ Proverbs 3:6

CONTENTS

FOREWORD

My name is Melanie. I have been a medium since birth. As with many of us "gifted" people, we cannot sometimes "read" for ourselves. So at one time I sought out another medium for guidance on how to find a channeling instructor in the area in which I lived. Instead, and much to my surprise, I was put in contact with Kevin Schoeppel, a very well-learned Biblical man and author. I thought to myself: *I ask for a channeling instructor and instead I get a Bible teacher? What's up with that?* I felt certain that this other medium had made a terrible mistake by putting me in touch with Kevin.

You and I perhaps have had similar experiences. Back in my youth I did not realize that not everyone could see and hear the things that I could. I am not sure at what age my grandmother told me to be silent and only share these types of things with her. But she did help me study anything we could find on metaphysical topics. And as I got older, I became braver and I began to talk to my other relatives about the things I had seen in a trance state. I would sometimes share with them the thoughts that came into my mind about certain people — thoughts that I knew were not my own. In doing so I knew they thought I was crazy or "touched." And yet, when my relatives and friends wanted explanations of unusual phenomena, such as orbs showing up in a photo that was taken with family members in it, they came to me seeking answers.

I sought out my own answers in many different ways, trying to find anyone or anything that could help me to understand why I was seeing spirits. And for explanations behind the things that had happened throughout my life, I read my Bible and whatever other books I could find. To this day I continue to educate myself on my spiritual gifts and on the supernatural in general.

I have fought so hard all of my life to get people to understand what it is like to be in my shoes, but after all, they are my shoes and no one else's. No one else can ever fully understand and my experiences will always be unique to me. And even if other people were to have the exact same experiences, their reactions would be different. But if through my gifts, I can at least speak to others about the love that God has for each of us, and what a gift it is to be alive then, yes, I have done the right thing.

Indeed, my willingness to bring forth messages for people has "bitten me in the butt" a few times. Why is it that people will question the heck out of me, get their answers and then turn around and use those answers against me later? I have also found it very peculiar that I am one of the ones these very same people call upon to join them in a prayer circle when someone is ill. Yet, the people who call upon me for this kind of help are the very ones who have also called me a witch or claimed that I am touched by evil, and say that they "worry about my soul." Heavens to Betsy, my soul is just fine. But if they could just give me a second I could tell them about the holes in theirs!

Why, I have even been asked by some people to put "jinxes" on other people — which I call hogwash and doing such things does not follow the teachings that I have learned from the Bible. For example, one such person came to me asking me to "put a spell on her husband" because he was cheating on her. I remember looking right at her and wanting to scream at her, "Now why would I ever do such a thing when I know you are sleeping with someone you work with?"

One morning a girl called me. I had known her for about eight years, and had done a reading for her for the first time about six months before. She used to tell me that she had thought that my doing such things was evil and ungodly. But that day she was calling to thank me because everything I had told her in the reading was one-hundred percent correct. And she said that it had changed her life for the better.

So here I was with this Bible teacher, Kevin, on the phone. I just knew for sure that he was going to eventually tell me he was "concerned about my soul." So in his first phone call to me, I told him what I do, and just waited for him to say it.

Instead, to my utter astonishment, what happened is that I got confirmation for my gifts of Spirit! At the time, certain family members had been calling me a witch. And I had been told by them that only men could foretell the future. But in our conversation Kevin pointed out to me that in the Bible God said:

"I will pour out my spirit upon all flesh; and your sons *and your daughters* shall prophesy." (Joel 2:28, KJV) I realized that as hard as I had previously tried to find validation, nothing meant more to me than these words that he quoted from the Bible, explained in a way that I could relate to and understand.

A trusting friendship soon developed between our families, and within a very short time I told him he needed to write a book. It happened one morning in the autumn of 2010. I sat up in bed to see what thoughts came to my mind. The thought I had was: *What if Kevin wrote a book that was meant to help people like me?*

Huh? What is this all about? I thought. It sounded terrific to me. I was at the point in my life where I was ready to take on the world since he had been teaching me how to trust the Bible. He had been showing me where it backs me up and others like me. But I knew that he might get more ridiculed than I when this book was finished.

Over the years, in the stories we have relayed to each other, I recalled the things that have been said about me and to me in past friendships, love relationships, and by distant family members.

Being tagged with certain names and labels has caused me incredible pain throughout my life. I knew I was not a witch. But just what was I mostly? I wondered how I do what I do, and I wondered if these gifts were blessed by God. *And what do I call myself?* I wondered.

Then one day Kevin said to me, "You are a gifted servant of the Lord." That made sense to me, for I have seen and felt the joy in people's hearts when they receive a message from a loved one on the "other side." At the same time, as a small town girl who was raised by her grandparents, being able to bring forth these messages from loved ones who have gone before also gives me a feeling of joy.

It seems that I keep mostly the same friends I have had all my life. I find that most of my friends do have a spiritual background or are Christians. But we all want our friends to love us no matter who or what they are. And so sometimes a psychic or medium will tend to feel that we can see a person's needs or situation more clearly than some of their other friends can, or that we are better equipped to "fix" their problems than someone else. But we don't realize at the same time that sometimes we are sometimes just being used.

We learn from these experiences and learn to weed them out in the future. Yes, we mediums get our feelings hurt just like anyone else does. That leaves many people asking the question: "If a medium is so psychic, then why aren't they able to know when they are being used?" We sometimes don't see it because we want don't want to see it. And we are all here to learn lessons in life. But in this process I have had to learn the art of discernment. These days if I cannot take someone's hand, bow my head, and praise God for the friendship then it is not for me.

Others ask, "Why don't psychics just pick the lottery numbers?" I believe that while some of us very well could, we are human also, and with a significant amount of additional money, we would perhaps do the same things as many non-mediums. So instead of continuing our spiritual growth and helping others with our gifts as we were meant to do, we could find ourselves focusing more on traveling, shopping, and acquiring possessions.

I admit that I do like being different. But I have lost many friendships throughout the years by mentioning the things I saw or felt. I have also gotten my heart broken in relationships by revealing too much about my gifts of Spirit.

For example, at the age of nineteen, when I returned home from spending three years at a private school in Mexico, I started to date a young man whom I had a large crush on for years. After three or four dates, one night I had a vision in which I saw him walking toward me while I was sleeping on the couch. In the vision, he had a very threatening look on his face, and I heard my Aunt Patty scream my name. It was a definite warning. The next time this man and I talked, I tentatively mentioned the vision I had had about him, and also told him many other things I had seen over the years. Immediately he stopped dating me.

In the late 1980s a young girl was kidnapped and murdered in our community. I had a pretty strong pull to a certain area of the town as to where I believed the child could be found. But I also knew that she was not alive anymore. However, there was no way I could have called 911 and told them, as I would have been tagged as a total nut. And since I was in the middle of a divorce at that time, I might have lost my children over it. I have always felt very guilty that I did not call in. The police might have found her body sooner than the years that it actually took them, and thus relieved the parents by giving them closure that much sooner.

Psychics are sometimes frightened of being judged by "Bible thumpers," as my grandma called them — the dear people who can quote the Bible verse by verse. This is mainly because we psychics have been judged and called all manner of names for doing what to us is simply just normal. To us the people who are *not* psychic are the ones that are not normal.

In the case of most "Bible people," for us to tell them that we sense things or are "psychic" is just asking to be told that we are going to Hell and need saving. And then they inevitably shove Bible verses at us. I bet you cannot truly name five people that are true Christians and believe in the Bible and spiritual gifts such as mine at the same time. For the most part they do not. Nor do I want someone to read or quote the Bible to me and tell me what it means. To me the Bible means different things to different people and my interpretation may be quite different from theirs.

Kevin has been correct in saying that people sometimes equate being a birth medium or a spiritually gifted person with being a witch. I have often been put into that category by others. We who are psychic desperately need help from the master teachers of the Bible who might instead explain like this:

> *Melanie, my name is Kevin, and you Melanie are psychic. I would love to talk to you about the Bible, because I would not just show you where the Bible supports your gifts, but I would show you how it can help you to accept and embrace your gifts. And you will ultimately see that the Bible cannot be twisted away from God's words.*

It has taken me many years to come to terms with my gifts. But finally knowing that I am fully supported by God and the Bible is the purest love I have ever felt. I hope this book will help change the stringent and erroneous attitudes held by many, and help people understand that there are indeed psychics and mediums with bona fide spiritual gifts from God.

Throughout my lifetime I tried several times to reach out to many people and different religions for "Biblical backing," which I never previously received prior to meeting Kevin. In that spirit it is my hope that this book also reaches the parents and families that find themselves now raising spiritually gifted children. These children may have been made to feel as if they are strangers in their own families, and may feel as if they must squelch or hide their gifts. It is my hope that they may not feel their gifts to be a curse as I did, but to be accepted as the special servants of the Lord that they are. In these challenging times we find ourselves living in, we need those with true spiritual gifts to be able to come forward freely and without judgment.

May no child ever from this day forward ever have to go through what I did. *Thank you, Kevin.*

INTRODUCTION

Why would I write a book like this? The answer is I've written it with the Lord's help and a desire to do His will. As long as I have known psychics, I've always been aware of how they have had to hide the special gifts that live within them simply out of public attitudes toward them.

First, there are the persons who simply refuse to believe in them. These are the people who think that all people who claim to be psychic are frauds. For them, no amount of proof will ever be enough. *Psychics are out to deceive you and take your money.* Furthermore, to them, any person who would believe in a psychic is a gullible fool.

Then, there are the persons who *do* believe in people who have psychic and psychic medium abilities — but with the belief that these persons have their abilities due to involvement in the occult or witchcraft. Because of certain verses in the Bible in which God commanded that the Israelites not consult persons who have "familiar spirits," and that there not be persons among them who practice divination, sorcery, witchcraft, and consulting of the dead, the churches of today have come to teach that all persons who have any extraordinary abilities are connected with the occult, and that all spirits who mediums communicate with are disguised demons.

Beyond that there are the misconceptions of what a psychic or medium can do. Thanks to the image that Hollywood and the media have created, much of the public believes that psychics should be able, at any time, to read anyone's thoughts, see into anyone's future, know any hidden information about a person, see any vision, know any tragedy that is about to happen, or have contact with the spirit of any dead person at will. And what if they can't on demand? *Oh, that certainly proves it — they're a fraud!*

So now let us assume that you are one of the specially gifted persons whom the Lord has graced with one or more of these extraordinary abilities. You learned quickly to keep your perceptions to yourself. You wanted to fit in and have friends. You didn't want your parents taking you to counseling. But there were so many times you wanted to share something you knew with your family or your friends that they had no other way of knowing, because you wanted to help them, warn them, or give them hope. You would think it over, and then invariably decide that you'd better not say anything at all.

As you got a bit older, you began to question why you are the way you are. You may have asked yourself: *Why can't I just be like everybody else? If there is a God who made all of us, why did he make me a 'freak?' Does he hate me?* All of your life you have just wanted to be a normal person like everyone around you.

Let us further assume that you are female. Although not all such gifted persons are female, I have found they greatly outnumber their male counterparts. As you went through your teens, there were boys that you liked. As you matured, you started developing deeper feelings in relationships. And then the questions started coming to your mind:

> *At what point do I tell him about my abilities? Do I tell him or do I just show him what I do? What if I can't keep it a secret and he discovers there is something 'weird' about me? Will his love for me change? Will he stay with me, or want to break off the relationship? What if his family has funny ideas about me and makes him choose between me*

and them? Will he freak out, run, and never want to see me again? Could my heart take that kind of rejection?

I have been that "boyfriend." Not just once, but twice. And what you have just read is based on what my wife Stanna, and my friend Melanie, and others have told me about what it's like to grow up with such psychic gifts. My heart has gone out to such persons from the time I met my first girlfriend, Tami, and discovered she was psychic. I wanted her to know I loved her for who she was, not for what she could do. And it's that very kind of acceptance that psychics and mediums long for to this day. Although I was afraid to ask questions directly to Tami about her abilities back then, I knew she had nothing to do with the occult. There was nothing evil about her or her conduct.

And so, after two assistant youth leaders at my church told me that I should stay away from Tami, because they assumed that her abilities were not from the Lord, I took a hard look at why I believed what I believed as far as a religion goes. No one was going to tell me to stay away from someone I loved just because she could do something the average person couldn't.

In the years since I've not only learned that such abilities can indeed be from the Lord, but that the Bible actually *supports* the fact that extrasensory abilities, and the ability to be contacted by spirits, are legitimate spiritual gifts. And because they are we have a responsibility to the Lord for the use of them. We are meant to serve the Lord with our spiritual gifts.

On the other hand, Christian churches today are hindering themselves by not accepting all spiritual gifts. "Quench not the Spirit. Despise not prophesyings. Prove all things; hold fast that which is good. Abstain from all appearance of evil." This is what

Kevin Schoeppel

their Bibles say in 1 Thessalonians 5:19-22 (KJV). *So why aren't any of them doing it?*

When was the last time someone in a church told you: "Stir up the gift of God, which is in thee?" That's in the Bible too, in 2 Timothy 1:6 (KJV). But let's say you didn't know what your gift is. How would you find out? In the early days of the Christian church, people with the gift of prophesy could tell you what your gift was. Okay, so where in the church is a person with this gift?

Sadly enough, one of two things may have happened. The person who had this gift may not be there anymore, because he or she felt they didn't belong. Instead of being encouraged to use their gift, they were shunned or were told they had a demon that needed to be cast out of them.

The other possibility is that the person with that gift is still there, but you wouldn't know it. They know what would happen if they were to let their gift be known to the church. So, since they love the Lord, and want to be a part of His church, they continue to hide their gift of prophesy. What an asset they could be — if only they could be assured of complete acceptance!

In the years that I taught Bible classes in the Baptist church, I've come to believe that the latter of these two possibilities is the more probable. Church members, like anyone else, experience extraordinary occurrences that they can't explain. And I've encouraged members of my class to talk about them. Of course, I first had to be willing to share a few unusual experiences of my own. Then they felt more at ease to tell me about theirs and ask their questions.

So there is a twofold purpose for this book. The first is for the spiritually gifted person to be able to understand where he or she stands with the Lord and with people, and to know what God commands them to do with their gift. And the second purpose is for the Christian church to become empowered, as the Lord intended for his church to be. They can accomplish this by reaching out in love to the psychic and medium, and creating an atmosphere of acceptance for all spiritually gifted people to openly serve God.

I have known from the time I began writing this book, that there will be plenty of opposition to the things I have written here. This book is full of verses and references from the Bible in regard to the subject matter. You will be able to see for yourself that these "strange" concepts are not some wild idea of mine. They are from the very book that is above all books — the book that much of the world has revered for almost two thousand years as being the all-sufficient, inerrant, word of God. But for those of you who are not of that opinion, I've also included a chapter titled "The Foundation of This Book: The Bible," in hopes that you will see what sets the Bible apart from all other holy books or writings.

So sit back. Ask the Holy Spirit for understanding. Turn the page. And prepare to be amazed.

ONE

Psychic Ability and Mediumship:
What God is Really Saying

Not long ago I received an email message through a popular social networking site from my former pastor's mother-in-law:

> *Kevin, have you checked the Word of God about mediums? The Bible has much to say about that. I hope you don't get involved in the occult. I pray the Holy Spirit will show you truth. Jesus is The Truth. Do your seeking in Him. I am praying for you.*

I wasn't sure what she had seen on my profile page that caused her to write this to me, but there were several good possibilities. I had several psychics and mediums on my friend list. And in my group page on the same social networking site, I had quite a few posts that dealt with the topic of mediums and psychics. I wasn't a skeptic. I wasn't seeking advice from them either. I was asking a lot of questions of them in order to understand more about their abilities, because I *did* know what God's Word had to say about psychics, as well as mediums.

I replied to her that I was aware of these five verses in the Bible, which most Christians will refer to when the subject of psychics, mediums, or the paranormal arises:

1. "Do not turn to mediums or spiritists; do not seek them out to be defiled by them. I am the Lord your God." — Leviticus 19:31 (NASB)

2. "As for the person who turns to mediums and to spiritists, to play the harlot after them, I will also set my face against that

person and will cut him off from among his people." — Leviticus 20:6 (NASB)

3. "Now a man or a woman who is a medium or a spiritist shall surely be put to death. They shall be stoned with stones, their bloodguiltiness is upon them." — Leviticus 20:27 (NASB)

4. "There shall not be found among you anyone who makes his son or his daughter pass through the fire, one who uses divination, one who practices witchcraft, or one who interprets omens, or a sorcerer, or one who casts a spell, or a medium, or a spiritist, or one who calls up the dead." — Deuteronomy 18:10-11 (NASB)

5. "When they say to you, "Consult the mediums and the spiritists who whisper and mutter," should not a people consult their God? Should they consult the dead on behalf of the living?" — Isaiah 8:19 (NASB)

These verses are enough to convince most Christians to stay away from anything paranormal. The verses seem to suggest that mediums deal with spirits that are not from God, and that it is a sin for any person to even associate with one. Some Christians even believe that by associating with a medium or a psychic, they will begin to turn away from serving God and start doing things displeasing to God.

This is what I believe that my former pastor's mother-in-law was concerned about. I had taught Sunday school classes and participated in many other church activities in her son-in-law's church. And now she was seeing on this social network that I had befriended several persons who were psychics and mediums.

What I already knew that she was unaware of, is that there are different ways in which these abilities are obtained. What makes

Kevin Schoeppel

the difference is the manner in which the person came to have the spiritual ability that they have.

So that you will understand what I'm talking about, let's take a closer look at the wording of those verses, and God's reasons behind his commands.

It's important for you to understand that the modern-day words used in those newer versions of the Bible don't always have the same meaning as the original words did at the time. So when a person reads a more up-to-date translation of the Bible other than the *King James Version*, be aware that some of the original intentions of the words have gotten distorted. The most pure translation, meaning, and intentions are found by referring to the *King James Version*.

Now, I have quoted the preceding five verses from the *New American Standard Bible*, which many churches use today. But back when the *King James Version* of the Bible was introduced in 1611, the word "medium" wasn't used in any of those verses. Instead, those same verses in the *King James Version* used the expression: "A man or a woman that has a 'familiar spirit'"— which actually is more specific than the word "medium." And the word "spiritist" was not used in the *King James Version* either, but rather what was used was the word "wizard."

And so what is a "familiar spirit?" And what is a "wizard?" To best define these terms with the meanings intended by the translators of the *King James Version* of the Bible, I used an 1828 *Webster's Revised Unabridged Dictionary*, available online. One definition of "familiar" is defined there as: "A demon or evil spirit supposed to attend at a call. But in general, we say, [sic] a familiar spirit." By this definition, a familiar spirit is contacted by the medium to serve the purpose of the medium. This would in turn imply that the medium makes the initial contact with the spirit. If the person with a "familiar spirit" made no effort to contact that spirit, there would be no action on the part of the spirit either.

In that same 1828 dictionary, *wizard* is defined as: "A conjurer; an enchanter; a sorcerer." By 1913, however, *Webster's Revised Unabridged Dictionary* had added to the definition of *wizard*: "A wise man; a sage." This was the intended meaning in the time of Thomas Edison, who was nicknamed "The Wizard of Menlo Park." And due to the technological advances in our century, the word "wizard" now has other meanings as well, such as in an "Internet connection set-up wizard." Thus our modern definitions of "wizard" now bear no resemblance to the true original meaning of the word.

The word *spiritist,* which did not appear in the 1828 dictionary edition, does appear in the 1913 edition and is defined there as: "A spiritualist." And so then if we look up the definitions of "spiritualist" in the 1913 edition here is what we find: "1. One who professes a regard for spiritual things only; one whose employment is of a spiritual character; an ecclesiastic. 2. One who maintains the doctrine of spiritualism. 3. One who believes in direct intercourse with departed spirits, through the agency of persons commonly called mediums, by means of physical phenomena; one who attempts to maintain such intercourse; a spiritist."

By being a deacon of a Baptist church, and teaching the spiritual truths of the Bible, that first definition of *spiritualist* — considered synonymous with "spiritist"— describes exactly what I do. So, in essence, the 20th-century Bible translators — by incorrectly choosing the word "spiritist" in place of "wizard"— now even make it forbidden by God for you to be consulting *me*.

However, let's now return to the issue of spirit contact. In both my studies of the Bible and from my personal experiences, there are persons *who have contact with spirits that they do NOT call upon.* To most of these persons, their very first encounter with anything supernatural happened at a very young age. For example, my friend, Melanie, was only four years old when she saw her grandmother's father standing near her grandmother's bed. (She identified him later by a picture).

We often hear accounts of young children seeing a person or spirit that others around them do not see. Although it is not impossible, it is very improbable that a child of that age would be interested in *calling on* spirits. Children of that age prefer playing with their toys or their friends rather than calling up spirits.

It is because of the Biblical warnings concerning persons who have a familiar spirit, that I make it a point to ask the psychics and mediums I meet if they were born with that innate ability to see and hear from spirits, or if they acquired that ability themselves in some way. Although such an ability can also be given to any of us at any time by the Holy Spirit, the majority of those who have involuntary spirit contacts have been having them since birth.

Melanie is one of these naturally gifted types of medium — a *birth medium*, as she calls herself. When I asked Melanie about her psychic gifts in 2010 shortly after I first met her, this was her answer:

> *I find it interesting that you are interested if I am a birth medium. I know it is from birth as I started so young. I had no exposure to bad or evil, only the Episcopal Church. I am forever grateful that my grandmother taught me that being a medium is not a bad thing, and to have a healthy respect and fear of it at the same time. Kevin, why is it that people do not realize it is a gift from God but also*

a curse to those who carry it? I truly believe God does not want me to be silent about it, but to acknowledge it.

There are spirits that make contact with us whether we are psychic or not. For example, Jesus taught that the Holy Spirit is one spirit who initiates contact with persons. In John 16:13-14 (NLT), he tells us: "When the Spirit of truth comes, he will guide you into all truth. He will not speak on his own but will tell you what he has heard. He will tell you about the future. He will bring me glory by telling you whatever he receives from me." Note that all of the actions are taken by the Holy Spirit, not the person. If the only type of spirit contact were by a person who has a familiar spirit — which is forbidden by God — then how do we account for the Scriptures in the *New Testament*, such as this one, that deal with spirit contact?

This ability to see and hear spirits can be part of any person whom the Holy Spirit chooses to bestow this gift upon. In Joel 2:28-29 (KJV), the Lord says: "And it shall come to pass afterward, that I will pour out my spirit upon all flesh; and your sons and your daughters shall prophesy, your old men shall dream dreams, your young men shall see visions: And also upon the servants and upon the handmaids in those days will I pour out my spirit."

Nothing in these verses says that prophesy, dreams, and visions only happen to those involved in the occult, or conversely only happen to those who are followers of Jesus Christ. God says: "I will pour out my Spirit upon all flesh."

By emphasizing that even servants, both men and women, would receive his spirit as well, God wanted us to know that he would make no class or social distinctions on who would receive the various supernatural abilities that the Spirit will give.

God wanted to make sure we understand that people who serve him in these times will also prophesy and have dreams and visions from the Lord. The sad part is that most Christians don't believe this, because they have not been taught to believe that God's Word said this will happen.

Psychic ability and mediumship which originate without effort on the part of the person, or which is given to one purely by the Holy Spirit, is as much of a spiritual gift from God as those spiritual gifts which the Bible expressly lists. And as is true of any supernatural ability, these gifts have their place and purpose in serving Christ.

In 1 Corinthians 1:5-7 (NLT), the Apostle Paul tells the church at Corinth: "Through [Christ], God has enriched your church in every way. . .now you have every spiritual gift you need." *Every* spiritual gift *does* include extrasensory abilities, and they are meant to be used along with those who have the more commonly acknowledged spiritual gifts, such as my own gift of teaching. By rejecting these types of gifts today, the Church is shortchanging itself.

I agree with Melanie that God does not want her to be silent about her gift. But for God's people to accept her gift, and those with similar gifts, to the same extent that they have accepted my teaching gift, and to benefit from her ability just as much as they have mine, will take some time and effort.

Let's go back to those five verses at the beginning of this chapter — Leviticus 19:31, Levitius 20:6, Leviticus 20:27, Deuteronomy 18:10-11, and Isaiah 8:19 — which are the core verses that form the basis of most Christian beliefs in the paranormal or extrasensory. Three of the five verses refer to *consulting, turning to, or following* "they that have familiar spirits, or a wizard."

The Lord does not want us to pursue this course of direction and this type of guidance. Why? In these verses are these types of persons themselves being called evil? Or will they "lure us into the Devil's trap?" No. The verses are directed to the person who would be *consulting or following the wizard, or person with a familiar spirit.* They are not directed to the "wizard," or the person having the "familiar spirit," who would be the object of the command.

Instead, the Lord tells us in Proverbs 3:5-6 (KJV): "Trust in the Lord with all thine heart; and lean not unto thine own understanding. In all thy ways acknowledge him, and he shall direct thy paths."

This trust is the kind of relationship with you that he wants. He directs that you not put your trust in someone with a psychic gift of precognition (that is, foretelling the future), but instead trust in God to guide you through the future that you do not know, *but that he does.*

If you had to make one choice — between either knowing the future, or trusting in someone greater than yourself who will guide and protect you through the future — which would you prefer?

When I previously taught a group of elementary school kids, I put it to them this way: "Suppose you hear a rumor that a big kid is waiting to beat you up on your way home from school one day. You ask some of your friends if they've heard if it's true or not. Some of them say, 'Yes.' Some of the others don't know. Then you ask one of your friends who is a really big, tough guy. He says, "I don't know, but I'll walk home from school with you." The future, like our past, contains both its good and bad moments. The Lord already knows all of them and is ready to direct your path.

But because our trusting relationship with the Lord is also based on obeying his commands, we should not do something that the Lord has said not to do. Deuteronomy 18:10-11(NASB) names several of these taboos. Keep in mind, as we take a closer look at the words used in those verses, that we must have a reasonable way to comply with God's commands:

- "There shall not be found among you anyone who makes his son or his daughter pass through the fire. . ." *We can choose to make our son or daughter pass through a fire or not.*

- "One who uses divination, one who practices witchcraft..." *We can decide whether we want to practice divination or witchcraft or not.*

- "One who interprets omens, or a sorcerer, or one who casts a spell. . ." *Likewise, it is up to us if we want to do these things or not.*

- "Or a medium, or a spiritist. . ." *If a medium or spiritist is what you have always been, how do you stop being yourself? Why would God ask such a thing of you?*

The truth is that he did not. When we read these same verses in the original *King James Version*, it says: "There shall not be found among you any one that maketh his son or his daughter to pass through the fire, or that useth divination, or an observer of times, or an enchanter, or a witch. Or a charmer, or a consulter with familiar spirits, or a wizard, or a necromancer."

The wording of the Bible in this version describes things that are all *practices,* which as you now know, cannot apply to the person who is not a psychic or medium by choice. All definitions of "wizard," as intended by the translators, *do* refer to a practice. And although in the *King James Version,* the phrase "practices witchcraft" changes to "a witch," it is already established that a witch is someone who *practices* witchcraft. And someone can choose to stop *practicing* witchcraft as well at any time.

A sin is something that you commit — not something that you *are.* In John 5:14, Jesus commands a man to stop sinning. You can stop engaging in a practice that is detestable to God, but you can't follow a command to quit being yourself.

If there were no other types of psychics or mediums besides a man or woman with a "familiar spirit," then how could we, or anyone, possibly obey the Bible's commands which deal with Spirit interaction in the *New Testament?*

In John 4:24 (NLT), we are told: "God is Spirit, so those who worship him must worship in spirit and in truth." We cannot avoid contact by spirits and worship God at the same time.

The Bible says in 1 Peter 3:19 (NLT), that Jesus "suffered physical death, but he was raised to life in the Spirit. So he went and preached to the spirits in prison." If Jesus himself preached the good news of the Kingdom of Heaven to spirits, how could he expect any follower of his to not have anything to do with spirits?

Jesus' followers were indeed communicating with spirits — because this warning is written in 1 John 4:1-3 (NASB): "Beloved, do not believe every spirit, but test the spirits to see whether they are from God, because many false prophets have gone out into the world. By this you know the Spirit of God: every spirit that confesses that Jesus Christ has come in the flesh is from God; and every spirit that does not confess Jesus is not from God." *Again, you cannot test spirits and avoid them at the same time.*

Jesus promised that the Holy Spirit would guide us into all truth, as I noted earlier. However, even in those times, there were religious people refusing the Holy Spirit. Stephen spoke these words to them: "You stiff-necked people with uncircumcised hearts and ears! You are always resisting the Holy Spirit!" (Acts 7:51, HCSB)

Jesus also commanded us to wait for the Spirit's power before doing any work for him. He said to his disciples in Luke 24:49 (NLT): "I will send the Holy Spirit, just as my Father promised. But stay here in the city until the Holy Spirit comes and fills you with power from heaven."

And later on he tells them: "You will receive power when the Holy Spirit has come upon you; and you shall be my witnesses both in Jerusalem, and in all Judea and Samaria, and even to the remotest part of the earth." (Acts 1:8, NASB)

So clearly, no Christian should avoid *all* spirits, nor avoid the people who have *contact* with spirits. We should not reject the Spirit's attempts to empower us and teach us. This is the reason why the Bible tells us to *test* the spirits, not to just reject them all as a way to avoid the evil ones. This is because when we reject spirit contact, we reject the Holy Spirit, and in turn we reject serving the Lord in the way he intended for us to serve him. For by resisting the Holy Spirit, we resist his guidance, his teaching, and his empowering us to serve.

However, whenever we set out to follow God's Word by reading it for ourselves, and understanding what it *really* says, we're going to get opposition. And it's not surprising that this opposition will come from the very people who claim to serve the Lord themselves.

I have noticed in my many years of church leadership that when questions are asked to Christian teachers about supernatural phenomena, the emphasis has been to generalize about the phenomena, and jump to easy conclusions about the origin of anything "supernatural."

I found one such example of this generalized mode of thinking on the Internet, in response to my search query: "What is the Christian view of psychics?" The answer in this article grouped together mediumship, the occult, psychic abilities, Tarot card reading, astrology, fortune telling, palm reading, and holding séances, as all simply being different variations of the same kind of supernatural ability.

Why generalize in this way? By asserting that all of these abilities and modalities are the same, the reader is asked to make one sweeping decision: Is God the source of the power behind all of these practices or not? The premise is that if even *one* of these practices is listed in Deuteronomy 18:10-11 as having been forbidden by God, then automatically *all* of them would have to be considered to be forbidden by God as well — *if* they truly are all variations of one and the same thing.

In this article that I found on the Internet, it is stated that the source of the phenomena is demons. And the Scripture passage 2 Corinthians 11:14-15, is then cited as the reason why, *but without quoting that verse in the article*. Why? It is because the writer's use of that passage is purposefully misleading.

In that passage (*New Living Translation*), it actually says: "Even Satan disguises himself as an angel of light. So it is no wonder that his servants also disguise themselves as servants of righteousness." So yes, the Bible says that Satan and his servants *can* be deceiving. But these verses do not really say that the source of *all* supernatural phenomena is Satan and his demons.

While the verses that I have quoted are a good reason why all psychics and mediums should test the spirits they come into contact with, there isn't a sufficient reason to assume that *all* of the spirits they encounter are demons. So we cannot summarily determine, as the writer of the article assumes, that demons are behind *all* supernatural abilities. Instead, we should always test any spirits we encounter.

One of the most common reasons many Christians directly assume that demons are masquerading as deceased loved ones, comes from the mistaken belief that the spirits of the deceased are either in Heaven or Hell at present, and can't possibly be on the Earth. As much as this concept is cherished by most Bible-believing Christians, *it is not biblical.* This is why the Bible does *not* say: "Have nothing to do with spirits, or you will be deceived by them," but rather, we are told to *test* the spirits.

Jesus told the Pharisees: "You completely invalidate God's command in order to maintain your tradition!" (Mark 7:9, HCSB) He was talking about the command, "Honor your father and mother." But we can say the same thing to our religious leaders of today about other commands of God.

In 1 Thessalonians 5:19-22 (HCSB), God commands us: "Don't stifle the Spirit. Don't despise prophecies, but test all things. Hold on to what is good. Stay away from every kind of evil." It seems that our churches and religious leaders of today are holding to a tradition of summarily "demonizing" the supernatural, instead of listening to what God's word is really saying about psychics, mediums, and spiritually gifted people.

Right before this verse tells us, "Hold on to what is good. Stay away from every kind of evil," it tells us to *TEST ALL THINGS.* If we don't test we can't hold on to the good. And that very "good" can often be found within the gifts of psychic ability and mediumship. When a psychic or medium shares their gifts with others who are differently gifted, they may very well bring forth exactly what is needed for a person's spiritual growth to occur as it should.

So why haven't we been testing, instead of listening to those who believe that all supernatural phenomena is evil? Who or *what* could be behind such a conclusion?

TWO

Enter the Confusion:
Christian Websites & the Bashing of Psychic Gifts

If God's Word says that we are supposed to test the spirits — which it does — and the early Christian church was communicating with spirits, why isn't this being done today? If we are supposed to accept all spiritual gifts that are from the Holy Spirit, including psychic and mediumship gifts, why do Christians now commonly believe that these abilities are from Satan or demons? Why am I one who seems to have a different view from that of the Christian churches? If I support everything I am saying with Scripture, and yet those opposed to mediums and psychics also seem to be supporting what *they* say with Scripture, then who is right?

These questions are important, because this indiscriminate denouncing of mediumship and all psychic abilities has caused the people who have always have had their abilities — such as my wife, Stanna — and who did not attempt to acquire them, to want to hide their gifts or ignore them, instead of using them to serve the Lord.

As I got to know Melanie better, she began to tell me of the times in her life where conventional Christian views about her gifts caused her pain in her relationships with others. A few months after we met, she wrote in an email to me:

> *At the age of sixteen I was allowed to date and I*
> *dated a young man named Bruce. He was such a*

kind young man, very religious, and even though my feelings went very deep for him, he wanted to fulfill his religious duties by going on a mission for his church. I had never shared with him my gifts of spirit because, from what I had learned, it was a big "no-no" in his religion. And I had already had many experiences already in losing someone I cared about by sharing that about myself.

+ + + + +

Even today, when information is so readily available to us in so many different ways, I have had difficulty in finding factual, straightforward information on psychic gifts and mediumship along with straightforward Biblical information.

If you go to a bookstore and look in the "Metaphysical" and "New Age" book sections, you find that most of those books contain no mention of the Lord Jesus Christ (for who he really is), and very few contain Scripture references supporting their information. Then, if you look in the "Christian" book section for books containing information on ESP, psychics, mediums, or the paranormal, most or all of the books you find there consider the source of each topic to be demonic or satanic, with no other possible point of view considered.

And if you search for these topics on the Internet, it's much the same thing. There are a lot of websites of mediums and psychics, with some calling themselves "psychic mediums." Unfortunately, on most of these sites there is most often no mention of the Lord Jesus Christ there, and most of the spiritual knowledge written about is based upon the firsthand experiences of the psychic or medium, or is based upon what has been passed on to them by other metaphysical practitioners. However, I *do* like reading what is on these websites because I have always been curious to know more about what it is like to be a psychic or a medium and to experience the abilities that they have.

It is these very curiosities that led me into social media initially, and to establish online friend relationships with several psychics and mediums. Social media then became my way to ask questions of these people, and to get answers firsthand, which I had previously been unable to do to any great extent. Many of these psychics were really quite surprised that a Christian would take an interest in them without condemning them or trying to get a reading.

+ + + + +

To discover answers to why most Christians have traditionally held firmly onto the dogmatic viewpoint of Satan or demons being the source of psychic and mediumistic abilities, I explored various Christian websites on the Internet. I did an Internet search on the keywords "God's Word," "psychics," and "mediums," and reviewed some of the search results. You can do this as well by going to any search engine, entering these same keywords, and clicking on the links to the various search results. Read for yourself what they have to say on some of these websites about psychics and mediums. Just as I expected, all of the websites I explored denounced all psychic phenomena and mediumship as satanic or demonic, just as the Christian books had as well.

In doing this search, I was seeking the *reasoning behind the views* regarding psychics, mediums, or anything supernatural that seemed to be held by the writers of these websites. Were their conclusions supported by the Bible? Did their reasons make logical sense? Or were their contentions of purported truth based solely on church teachings that, while persuasive enough to *appear* Biblical, were not truly supported by the Bible?

As I browsed the search results that I found, I took note of what kinds of logical techniques these websites commonly used in support of their conclusions. Strangely enough, but not surprisingly to me, was that if or when these websites referred to the Bible to make their point, the verses which they referred to actually *didn't* support what the writer was attempting to say.

Here are the techniques frequently used not just on websites, but in other venues as well, to support the premise that the abilities psychics and mediums have are from an evil source. And you will find that you come to understand why such reasoning does not hold up:

- Generalizing
- Incorrect definition
- Authority without being held accountable to authority
- Misapplication of Scripture
- Flawed logic
- Added teachings

The first of these techniques, and the most common, is generalizing, Generalizing is frequently used to persuade people that *any* supernatural ability that a person may be gifted with is all the same thing, no matter what it is called.

The second of these techniques is what I call "using incorrect definition." Previously I cited an early edition of *Webster's Revised Unabridged Dictionary* to provide you a correct definition of a "familiar spirit" and a "wizard" as used in the *King James Version* Bible. On one of these Christian websites, however, I read

Kevin Schoeppel

a totally different definition. That website defined a "consulter with familiar spirits" as being "a medium or a séance leader" — but without citing any authoritative, defining source, including a dictionary.

Incorrect definitions of terms used in the Bible has led many Christians to misunderstand their own Bible, has led many psychics and mediums to believe that God hates them, and has kept both groups from considering that there may be persons who are naturally and fundamentally gifted with extrasensory perception whom the Bible does not condemn.

The third technique, sometimes based solely on the credentials or reputation of the author or speaker, is what I call "authority without being held accountable to authority." This is the making of statements *without any Scriptures or authoritative definitions to support their allegations.*

At one Christian website, I read — *without one authoritative reference to support the truth of such things* — that psychics and mediums (a) pretend to be in tune with God (b) have placed their souls in danger, and (c) possess abilities from Satan. On the same website I also read that *only* our Creator knows our future, but the article failed then to furnish any supporting Scripture for that viewpoint.

God certainly knows our future, as Isaiah 44:7-8 tells us. However, in Amos 3:7, we also read that God does nothing without revealing his plans to his servants, the prophets. So how can it be asserted then that *only* God knows our future, if he reveals it to prophets? Sometimes, God even reveals the future to persons who *aren't* his prophets — *just to test us.*

As an example of this, in Deuteronomy 13:1-3 (NASB), the Bible says: "If a prophet or a dreamer of dreams arises among you and gives you a sign or a wonder, and the sign or the wonder comes true, concerning which he spoke to you, saying, 'Let us go after other gods (whom you have not known) and let us serve them,' you shall not listen to the words of that prophet or that dreamer of dreams; for the Lord your God is testing you to find out if you love the Lord your God with all your heart and with all your soul."

The fourth technique that is often employed on Christian websites, to make the point that all psychics and mediums are evil, is misapplication of Scripture. In one example, 2 Corinthians 11:14-15 (NLT), which I mentioned earlier, is the Scripture reference used as the writer's reasoning to "prove" that mediums communicate with demons. But if you look up those verses in the *New Living Translation* of the Bible, here is what it says: "Even Satan disguises himself as an angel of light. So it is no wonder that his servants also disguise themselves as servants of righteousness." We only read here that Satan or demons *could* masquerade as an angel of light or as a servant of righteousness — *not* that all spirits contacting mediums *were or are* demons.

Whenever someone gives you any religious teaching, and does not teach it directly from the Bible, simply ask the person, "Can you show me where it says this in the Bible?" They will probably not know the Scripture reference and will tell you, "I don't know exactly *where* it says that, but I just *know* it is in the Bible." Or they will lead you to a Scripture that is meant to support their view, but when you look up this Scripture, you discover that it has nothing to do with their teaching.

At another Christian website I visited, I read that when a person goes to a medium, a psychic, or a spiritualist, that they are "playing with fire and opening themselves up to demon possession." The one-chapter book of Jude, verses 8-9 was then cited to support the reasons why.

However, if you actually go to the book of Jude, which is the second to the last book of the Bible, and spend five minutes to read it, you will find nothing whatsoever mentioned in any of its twenty-five verses about psychics, mediums, or demons. You will, ironically, find a discussion about godless men who "sneaked in" amongst Christians to speak evil about things that they don't understand, and are complainers and fault-finders. Jude goes on to say that these godless men follow their instincts and not the Spirit.

Another website I came upon had an article that announced: "The Bible makes it very clear where mediums and psychics' power comes from." The writer of that article pointed to Acts, chapter 8, which tells the story of a person, Simon the Sorcerer in Samaria. But nowhere in that story does the Bible claim that Simon had psychic or mediumistic abilities. So no, the Bible does *not* "make it very clear." The Bible, in reality, gives us tests and commands us to test everything *because* it is not necessarily always a clear-cut case as to the source of these abilities.

When you encounter anyone who says that they have Scripture that proves that a medium or psychic's ability does not come from the Lord, know that very likely they will quote you one of the five Scripture passages I immediately addressed in the first chapter on pages 19 and 20. Those are the most commonly used in any Christian discussion of psychic abilities or mediumship. But if other Scriptures are used to prove that mediums or psychics abilities are not from the Lord, it's important to note that *those verses may not have anything to do with mediums or psychics at all.* The best thing you can do is look it up yourself.

A fifth technique I found that is often used on Christian websites to discredit psychics and mediums is flawed logic. This simply means that the argument can't make logical sense when you apply logic to it. For instance, I read on one of these websites that God considered psychics and mediums to be an abomination because anyone who went to a psychic or medium wasn't relying on God for guidance. This does not make sense. What makes a person good or evil is their *own* actions, *not someone else's* actions.

I once visited the website of the Witches' League for Public Awareness to find what witches believed in. One of these beliefs I read is that witchcraft is a religion that allows a personal relationship with each person's concept of deity. Does someone's *concept* of God make God what they think he is? Can two witches with opposite concepts of God *both* be right about who God really is? Can God even be two different things at the same time?

Furthermore, what about me? If someone reads this book and calls me a heavenly messenger and claims I wrote the "new Bible," does that perception make me abominable in God's sight? And if someone else has the viewpoint that I must be a messenger of Satan because my book validates the gifts of mediums and psychics, does that really make me evil? Can I in actuality be a messenger of both evil and good just because two readers see me differently? Others can have differing opinions of what we are, *but we can't be both evil and good at the same time.*

A less obvious flaw in logic, as I found on another Christian website, is to declare that the whole Bible is the perfect, inerrant, Word of God, but then go on to say about any part of the Bible that, "These scriptures do not apply to us today," if the verses didn't fit *their* beliefs.

Here is an example of what I found on this website: "Use of spiritual messengers by God — prophets, angels, and seers — ended in biblical times." If spiritual messengers really ended in Biblical times, then why does the Bible command us to desire the gift of prophecy? 1 Corinthians 14:1 (NLT) says: "Desire the special abilities the Spirit gives — especially the ability to prophesy."

If it is left up to men to decide what parts of the Bible are valid and what parts are obsolete and outdated, then one man's opinion is as good as another's. You either believe the Bible is accurate and relevant or that it is not. No person, no matter how highly educated, has sufficient education to unilaterally decide that there are some Biblical teachings we should obey and others which we should disregard.

Ironically, the sixth technique sometimes used by Christian websites, is to add to teachings which are not stated in the Bible, and then try to persuade their readers to accept these teachings as authoritative. For example, on one of the websites I found, it was discussed at length how "psychic ability is developed."

There aren't any verses in the Bible on developing psychic ability, or on how to develop *any* spiritual gift. None of the psychics I have known personally ever initially received their ability by working to develop and garner what they did not previously have.

Being taught and growing in the Spirit, however, is a different issue from developing psychic abilities or any other spiritual gift — and the Bible *does* have teachings on spiritual growth. 1 John 2:27 (NLT) says: "You have received the Holy Spirit, and he lives within you, so you don't need anyone to teach you what is true. For the Spirit teaches you everything you need to know, and what he teaches is true." And in John 16:12-13 (NLT), Jesus said: "There is so much more I want to tell you, but you can't bear it now. When the Spirit of truth comes, he will guide you into all truth."

Non-Biblical added teachings tend to gain acceptance with Christians when these attempt to "fills in the gaps" to fit church beliefs on anything which the Bible is silent about. Surprisingly perhaps, the most controversial lesson I ever taught in a Sunday school class was not about spiritual gifts. Nor was it about when or how the world will end. It was the story in John, chapter 2 about Jesus turning water into wine at a wedding feast in Cana.

What makes it such a controversial lesson is that most Christians can't accept the fact in their minds that Jesus miraculously created an alcoholic beverage. And so they say that the word translated as "wine" really means "grape juice" or a wine without alcoholic content. Others perhaps want to give some cultural reason why Jesus would provide wine. But the Bible never says whether the wine was non-alcoholic or not. Nor does it tell us why Jesus performed this miracle. We are merely told that, according to the one in charge of the wedding feast, the servants had kept the best wine saved for a time that ordinarily would have been the time to set out cheaper wine, since the guests had already partaken of the better wine. These are the facts, given without reasons, as to why the actions were done. In James 1:21 (NLT), we are commanded to "humbly accept the word God has planted in your hearts." And we must recognize that we can't *add* something to Scripture to make it fit our own beliefs.

Further, we can't say definitively, as I read in yet another article on a Christian website, that the reason young children have psychic or spirit encounters is because the child or his parents visited a psychic, dabbled in the occult, or used Ouija boards. The author of that article did not support his theory with any case studies, history, or facts. Whereas, my own experiences have shown me exactly the opposite: That no family members' actions brought about their child's psychic or supernatural abilities. I have found, however, that with most persons gifted with psychic or medium abilities from birth, a relative also was gifted with such abilities, even if they actively used their gifts or simply chose to keep silent and hide them. Melanie has attested to the fact that her grandmother had been gifted also, and I have personally observed my son's supernatural gifts, along with my wife's. *All three of these persons had no family members involved in occult activity.*

+ + + + +

While I was doing my research for this chapter, I came across this disturbing question, which begged for an answer. It was posted in an online forum by a young woman:

> *Why does God give people psychic abilities if he hates those who engage in it? I believe that I have psychic abilities and saw something today that says God hates people who engage in psychic things or talks to spirits. I was just wondering though why he gives people "gifts," if he even killed Saul because Saul consulted the dead. It doesn't even make sense to call it a gift if it's more like a curse. Please answer me because it would mean a lot to me.*

The question was posted more than two years before I read it. Otherwise, I would have answered the woman who wrote this. I would have told her that God does *not* hate her. The second thing I would have done is to ask her questions about her psychic abilities:

How long have you had these abilities? And what, if anything, did you do to become psychic or be able to communicate with spirits?

If she had done anything to try to acquire the gifts or develop the gifts, I would have said that it's time for her to stop. I would have shown her Deuteronomy 18:10 and explained that God does not want us to engage in these practices that he has told us not to engage in. I would have told her that God hates disobedience, not the person.

But if the woman had always remembered being psychic, or could say that she never did anything to *become* psychic, then I would tell her the Lord made her that way for a special purpose, and that purpose is to serve him with that ability.

Jesus did not say in John 3:16: "For God so loved the world. . . *except psychics and mediums.*" And his disciple Peter wrote in 2 Peter 3:9 (NASB): "The Lord. . . is patient toward you, not wishing for any to perish but for all to come to repentance." Yes, *any.* That means *everyone.* That includes all persons, psychically gifted or not. And Paul wrote in Romans 8:1 (NLT): "There is no condemnation for those who belong to Christ Jesus." No exceptions were made for psychics or mediums.

Are psychically gifted persons the object of God's wrath? Actually, we all are — or *were.* The Bible says in Ephesians 2:3-7 (NLT): "By our very nature we were subject to God's anger, just like everyone else. But God is so rich in mercy, and he loved us so much, that even though we were dead because of our sins, he gave us life when he raised Christ from the dead. It is only by God's grace that you have been saved! For he raised us from the dead along with Christ and seated us with him in the heavenly realms because we are united with Christ Jesus. So God can point to us in all future ages as examples of the incredible wealth of his grace and kindness toward us, as shown in all he has done for us who are united with Christ Jesus."

If God loves *all of us* so much, then why do the majority of Christians and Christian websites seem so quick to jump to the unsupported conclusion that any psychic or medium must be demon-possessed, that their power comes from Satan, or that all

Kevin Schoeppel

the spirits they are in contact with are really demons? I really don't know. I could make several guesses, but instead let me point out Scriptures that may reassure you that you're in good company. You might be surprised to know that some of the religious leaders in Jesus' time considered John the Baptist to be demon-possessed. In Luke 7:33 (HCSB), Jesus said to the Pharisees: "John the Baptist did not come eating bread or drinking wine, and you say, 'He has a demon!'"

You might be shocked to know that these same religious leaders considered Jesus' power to come from demons, too. Mark 3:20-22 (NLT) says: "One time Jesus entered a house, and the crowds began to gather again. Soon he and his disciples couldn't even find time to eat. When his family heard what was happening, they tried to take him away. 'He's out of his mind,' they said. But the teachers of religious law who had arrived from Jerusalem said, 'He's possessed by Satan, the prince of demons. That's where he gets the power to cast out demons.'"

Another time, in John 8:48 (HCSB), the Bible tells us that the Jews asked Jesus: "Aren't we right in saying that you're a Samaritan and have a demon?"

And even at a different time and place, in John 10:20 (NLT), we read this said about Jesus: "He's demon possessed and out of his mind. Why listen to a man like that?"

Jesus even predicted that his followers would also be called "evil" or "demon-possessed" by the religious leaders of today. He said in Matthew 10:25 (NLT): "Students are to be like their teacher, and slaves are to be like their master. And since I, the master of the household, have been called the prince of demons, the members of my household will be called by even worse names!"

We read in John 16:1-3 (NLT), that Jesus also said: "I have told you these things so that you won't abandon your faith. For you will be expelled from the synagogues, and the time is coming when those who kill you will think they are doing a holy service for God. This is because they have never known the Father or me."

Yes, Jesus knew long ago that when respected religious leaders call you "evil" or "demon-possessed" because of your psychic gift, it can naturally cause you to have your doubts. You might have even been led into thinking — like the woman who posted her question in the online forum — that maybe God really does hate you because of your gift. Jesus doesn't want you to be confused by the persons who want you to believe that supernatural abilities do not come from God

+ + + + +

Several years ago, I took a pastor to task on the issue of why, if Jesus used ESP abilities, did that pastor consider such abilities to be demonic? The man's first response was that Jesus didn't use ESP. So already he and I weren't on the same "page." To me, ESP was simply the abbreviation for "extrasensory perception"— receiving information without the normal five senses. To the pastor, ESP was a *source,* such as God or the Devil, of the information received without the senses.

The pastor went on to quote the scripture John 5:19, to tell me that without God the Father supplying Jesus' abilities only for specific times and instances, Jesus was powerless. In fact, however, the verse doesn't say that at all about Jesus' abilities. It merely states that the Son does nothing on his own, but does what he sees the Father doing. The verse is about *obedience,* not *power.*

When I didn't accept the pastor's first answer, he moved on to *his* "test" for the source of ability which was: *If we have to wait for*

God to tell us when to use an ability, then it is from the Holy Spirit. And if we can use an ability at will, it is demonic. Not only does his test not appear anywhere in Scripture, but he failed to refer me to the true Biblical test — the one in 1 John 4:1-3, which says that every spirit that confesses that Jesus is God in the flesh is of God. There is *no* other Biblical test of a spirit.

The Apostle Paul wrote in 1 Corinthians 14:33 (KJV): "God is not the author of confusion, but of peace."

And so who really is the author of confusion?

THREE
Love Makes the Difference

The word "bewitched" appears only once in the Bible. In Galatians 3:1 (NASB), it says: "You foolish Galatians! Who has bewitched you?" "Bewitched" was not used in relation to witchcraft or magic in the book of Galatians, but rather to confusion. Later in the book of Galatians, Paul writes: "Who prevented you from obeying the truth? This persuasion did not come from the One who called you. I have confidence in the Lord you will not accept any other view. But whoever it is that is confusing you will pay the penalty." (Galatians 5:7-8, 10, HCSB)

This very thought, which came to me from the Spirit of the Lord as I prepared to write, struck me as very ironic. How unusual was it that the persons whom the Bible calls "bewitching" are the very people who attempt to call psychics and mediums "witches."

Of course, to people today, the word "bewitched" may bring to mind the classic 1960s TV series about a man, Darrin, who married a beautiful witch, Samantha. Darrin didn't find out that she was a witch until their wedding night. Initially it was a shock to him, but after thinking it over, he said to her in that first episode, "I've come to a decision. I love you and can't give you up."

Right now, picture in your mind someone you love or have loved. It could be a parent or grandparent, or any another person who loved and cared for you as you grew up, such as an aunt or uncle, or a close friend of the family. Or it could be a person you're in love with now as a boyfriend or girlfriend, or a husband or wife. Think about all of the times that this special person you love so much just happened to have a way of "knowing" things about you.

Kevin Schoeppel

Maybe it was something you thought no one else knew about except you. Maybe it was something you did when no one else was around, but your loved one just seemed to know somehow. If you asked them how they know or knew, and they just smiled and answered you with, "Oh, I have my ways," or "A little bird told me."

And now think about the times when something has troubled you. And you might have wished you could know what to do about it or what to say so that someone else would understand. Maybe it wasn't even about you, but someone else you cared about. And you found that this special person would come to you, put their arm around you, hold you closely and gently ask, "Want to talk about it?"

You never quite understood how they just happened to know these things. You might have thought about it from time to time, and wondered about it, but it really didn't matter to you. They just have or had a knack or ability to know, and you have just always known that about them and accepted it. They are a special person to you, and to think of them now brings a smile to your face and pleasant memories to mind of your times with them.

Now let's say that along comes a time later on in your life when you're doing something socially with friends, and for some reason the subject of psychics comes up. Maybe someone is telling a story, or a television commercial comes on for a "psychic hotline." Let's imagine now that someone says to you, "I've heard that people who do that stuff are messing around with the Devil or evil spirits." Stop and notice your reaction. You might calmly disagree with the person who says that, or you might get very defensive. But you will discover that your mind is rejecting the notion that your special loved one has or ever had anything to do with the Devil.

Why? It's because of your special love for that person. And you remember all of those special times when they were there for you. Just how could someone you love so much, and who loves you just the same, have anything to do with demons?

In 1 Corinthians 13:7 (NASB), The Bible says that love "bears all things, believes all things, hopes all things, and endures all things." The Apostle Paul understood this, as he said in Galatians 5:19-23 (NASB): "Now the deeds of the flesh are evident, which are: Immorality, impurity, sensuality, idolatry, sorcery, enmities, strife, jealousy, outbursts of anger, disputes, dissensions, factions, envying, drunkenness, carousing, and things like these, of which I forewarn you, just as I have forewarned you, that those who practice such things will not inherit the kingdom of God. But the fruit of the Spirit is love, joy, peace, patience, kindness, goodness, faithfulness, gentleness, self-control; against such things there is no law."

And Matthew 7:16-18 (HCSB), we read that Jesus said: "You'll recognize them by their fruit. Are grapes gathered from thorn bushes, or figs from thistles? In the same way, every good tree produces good fruit, but a bad tree produces bad fruit. A good tree can't produce bad fruit; neither can a bad tree produce good fruit." Jesus used the simple example of fruit from a tree, but because he is referring to false prophets back in verse 15 which precedes these verses, he was more likely referring to the fruit of the Spirit that he knew Paul would write about later.

+ + + + +

I can still remember the day I posed a question to a youth leader at my church when I was seventeen. "What do you think of someone who knows something is going to happen before it happens?" I asked.

His answer: "That is not something of the Lord. I would stay away from them."

I felt that he was trying to tell me this ability comes from the Devil, without actually saying so. Even at that time in my life, I believed that such an ability didn't have to come from the Lord or Satan, but that it could be a natural part of a person, just as much as an arm or leg. What I didn't tell him was that this "someone" I was asking about was a fifteen-year-old girl right in the same youth group of the church. And with that kind of response, I was glad I didn't.

This conversation was approximately a year after the movie *The Exorcist* had been in the theatres, and when ESP or something supernatural was the topic, demonic possession was still fresh in the minds of most people. The question on my mind whenever anyone discussed the movie back then was:

Why does everyone think that everything supernatural has to come from the Devil? Why can't it come from God? We're told to pray to God, to believe in God, but when it comes to anything that happens out of the ordinary, that's from the Devil. Doesn't God have any power at all?

When we love someone or someone is special to our lives, our natural inclination is to accept them and love them as they are. If they are our children, we guide their growing up with discipline, which is in turn guided by our love for them. We protect and defend them from anyone who would do them harm.

As the Bible says in 1 Corinthians 13:5-6 (NLT): "Love is patient and kind. Love is not jealous or boastful or proud or rude. It does not demand its own way. It is not irritable, and it keeps no record of being wronged. It does not rejoice about injustice but rejoices whenever the truth wins out."

Well, this particular girl, Tami, was very special to me. She was my first girlfriend and I was her first boyfriend.

+ + + + +

It was about a month before I had questioned the youth leader that the young lady, Tami, and I were at an overnight youth retreat on Mt. Lemmon, near Tucson, Arizona. The sun had gone down and I decided to go back to the cabin and put my camera away before our chapel services. I noticed that Tami was following me, and she asked me where I was going.

"Just going up to put my camera away," I replied.

"I'll hold it for you," she said brightly.

So I handed it over to her, and then I watched her walk down a side path over to a concrete slab that housed a water tank for the camp. She sat down on the slab. I followed and sat down beside her on her right. From this vantage point we could see the twinkling lights of the city of Tucson far below. The full moon had just risen over the mountains to the east of us. The stars shone brilliantly and there was the cool, fall breeze in the air, which rustled softly through the pines.

"It's so beautiful up here," she said softly.

Have you ever had one of those moments when you just don't know what to say? Feeling the awkwardness of youth, I was momentarily silent as I gazed toward the distant lights of Tucson. Then I said, "I wonder who's winning the football game down there?"

Her reply wasn't really what I was expecting — if I really was expecting anything in particular at all.

"I already know. Rincon's going to lose."

Rincon was my high school, and so I took this as some sort of a taunt. I replied, "And just what makes you think so?"

"Because Palo Verde's going to win," she said with conviction.

"But they're not playing each other!" I exclaimed. Palo Verde was her high school, but her answer seemed like nonsense to me.

"Look," she said, "every time Rincon wins, Palo Verde loses. And every time Rincon loses, Palo Verde wins."

I thought back over the five past weeks since the high school football season had begun. *She's right,* I thought. I didn't really follow football, but I remembered what I had heard around school, and from some friends at Palo Verde. Still, something inside me told me this way of thinking just had to have a flaw in it. Anything this weird had to. And just then I thought I had found it.

"What about when our schools play each other in three weeks?" I asked her. "Your theory won't hold water then, because obviously, if one wins, the other loses," I said. "So who's going to win then?"

She turned and looked up at the stars, got that mischievous look in her eyes, and smiled that knowing smile that I would get accustomed to seeing many times in the future. "Mmmm..." she replied. "Neither one!"

"What do you mean, 'neither one?'"

"Just what I said. Neither one!"

I just stared at her in silent astonishment. It was time to go, so we both scrambled up quickly from the concrete slab. We said nothing more about it as we made our way to the camp chapel, the silvery full moon illuminating our pathway.

+ + + + +

Monday morning, back at school, I found out Rincon really had lost on Friday night. And that afternoon I found out that Palo Verde had won their game — exactly what Tami said would happen.

The next week, the same thing happened. One of the schools lost their game and the other one won theirs. The following week was Halloween, and her theory being correct for the third week in a row was now spooking me even more. Next week would be the one in which our schools would play each other. So just what did she mean by saying "neither one" would win? What was supposed to happen?

I was at a friend's house on the Friday afternoon before the game. He attended Palo Verde, and so he asked me who I thought was going to win between our two schools. "I don't mean to be disloyal," I said, "but I think Palo Verde's going to win this one." But then I told him of Tami's prediction.

He gave me a quizzical, dumbfounded look. "Neither One? What's that supposed to mean?"

"That's what I said," I told him. "All she said was that she meant just that — neither one."

I had to work that night. My boss was reluctant to let high school kids take Friday nights off, and I had already gotten time off for the church camp weekend three weeks ago. But after work I drove back over to my friend's house. He saw me pull up, and ran like a gazelle across the street to greet me as I got out of the car.

"IT WAS A TIE! IT WAS A TIE!" He excitedly began telling me how Rincon was leading at the halftime 6-0, and how the game stayed that way until Palo Verde scored a touchdown with only thirty seconds to go in the fourth quarter, tying the game. He went on about how the pressure was on for the extra point, but the kick was no good. The game was over, ending in a tie. It hadn't occurred to me that because high school football did not permit overtime except in playoffs, it really was possible for a game to end in a tie. I just hadn't seen it happen in any of my four years in high school — until now.

So that's what Tami meant by 'neither one,' I thought. It didn't take long for me to guess what the odds must be against a game ending in a tie, and yet she knew it three weeks previously when we were on Mt. Lemmon. For the rest of the evening, I kept pondering over and over in my thoughts: *How did she know?*

The next day I received two different phone calls at home from people I didn't know. "Are you the one who has the girlfriend who predicts football games? Can you ask her who's going to win Palo Verde's game next week?" I told both of them I was not going to ask her anything.

When I saw Tami later, she said, "Tell your friends to stop calling me."

I told her that the ones calling her weren't any of my friends, and besides that I had gotten two calls myself asking for game predictions. But I still was curious how she did know, and so I asked her.

She simply said, "I don't know. I just know."

I didn't want to drive her away by prying, so I left it at that. Every once in a while, I would ask her in a different way, hoping I would somehow find out how she was able to know. But she always had her own evasive answer. I never really did find out anything from her about her abilities, but this was the Lord's way to begin to prepare my ways of thinking for the future ahead.

Kevin Schoeppel

FOUR

From There to Here

I felt a sense of embarrassment for the phone calls Tami had received. The only way I imagined that they could have happened was for my friend from Palo Verde to have told someone else before the game about Tami's prediction that neither team would win. And so, I resolved to myself that afternoon, November 8, 1975, that I would never ask for a prediction.

But I couldn't stop being curious about how she could know things before they happened. In the back of my mind, I started keeping track of when she said something would happen. For the next two years, until I met Stanna in July, 1977, there were a total of eighteen times my former girlfriend would say something was going to happen. And all eighteen times her predictions came true.

I had read stories about ESP, and had even listened to a radio program about it over a year earlier. But I had never personally known anyone who could do these things. And now I was in love with one! For two reasons I had already firmly rejected the notion in my mind that her ability wasn't from the Lord. Nor did I believe that I should stay away.

First, when you love someone, your mind won't accept that their abilities come from the Devil. Second, how could Christians believe in all of the supernatural things that Jesus did, and that his disciples did in the book of Acts, but then say that anything supernatural today must not be from the Lord? Why couldn't it be? It made no sense to me.

And so at eighteen, for the first time, I began to seriously ask myself why I believed what I claimed to believe, pertaining to a religion or a belief in God. Did I have a reason for my beliefs, or were my beliefs only a result of the way I was raised? Because for the first time, I was having a conflict between what I was taught and what I was experiencing first-hand. And although I had been to a Bible teaching church all of my life, I had almost no real knowledge about ESP.

The University of Arizona, where I was enrolled in the fall of 1976, had copies of *Parapsychology Review* in their serials department in the basement of the library. These seemed to be the most factual sources of information on ESP that I could find. I would read them between classes. I was by now well past any doubts that ESP abilities existed.

As part of a research paper I was writing for my English class, I was referencing that publication. I had chosen to research social reactions to people with psychic abilities. In the 1970s, however, most literature on ESP mainly dealt with proving its existence. And so I had to do some original research, which my instructor pre-approved as a source for my paper.

At that time I delivered pizza on weekend nights. Sometimes when I would deliver to a group of people staying at a motel, I'd ask them if they would be willing to take a short survey I was doing for a research paper. They would always be ready to help me out. I would also ask people at my work, my church, in my other classes, and even a few customers who dropped in for a pizza. I really can't remember anyone refusing. Both the research notes and the research paper are long gone, but I will share with you what I remember from doing that original research.

My initial questions were:

- Do you believe in psychic abilities?

Kevin Schoeppel

- Have you ever wanted to know more about psychic abilities?
- Have you ever read any books or information on psychic abilities?
- Have you ever known someone with psychic abilities?
- If so:
    (a) Have you wanted to know more about their abilities?
    (b) Or you didn't want to know more about their abilities?
    (c) Or do you not care?

So in a few days, I had fifty responses and thought back over the people whom I had questioned for my paper. About half were strangers, and half were people I knew. About half were younger people, and about half were older persons. About half were women, and half were men. By stopping at fifty, I felt I had a pretty good cross-section of people, and to keep the math simple, every individual statistically represented 2%. Here were my results:

- 64% (thirty-two people) believed in people having psychic abilities.

- 36% (eighteen people) did not.

- 62% (thirty-one people) wanted to know more about psychic abilities. 38% did not.

- 16% (eight people) knew someone with psychic abilities.

- And of the eight, 10% (five people) were curious to know more about the person's abilities, and 4% (two people) didn't care to know any more about such abilities. But one person of the eight said he was afraid of the person with such abilities.

- Only 8% (four people) had ever read books or information on psychic abilities.

Interestingly, the one person who answered that he was afraid of the psychic he knew happened to be my friend from Palo Verde, to whom I had told the "neither one" prediction to a year earlier.

What really was significant to me about that survey was that although 62% of all people were curious to know more about psychic abilities, only 8% ever bothered to educate themselves by reading or seeking out any books or information on the subject. And so it seemed to me that a lot of what people "knew" about psychics wasn't based on any informational sources, but just what they had "heard."

Upon completing the research paper I concluded that psychics were a group of people being discriminated against. It was just like discrimination because of race, color, sex, creed, or national origin, but with two basic differences. First, you only knew if a person was psychic if they somehow revealed their abilities. But then once discovered, there would still be an issue of whether they would be believed or taken seriously. They could still be considered crazy, delusional, or a fraud.

Psychics just wanted to be treated like everyone else, I thought. *They want to have friends who accept them for who they are, and not act like they're some novelty or party entertainment. And they never want to not be taken seriously in the real world. . .and especially they do not want to be viewed as demon-possessed!*

Meanwhile, at about that same time, a Christian apologetics speaker, Josh McDowell, came to speak at the University of

Arizona. I went to one of his presentations in the main auditorium, which dealt with the reasons why we can trust the Bible to be God's Word. For the first time in my life, I realized I did not have to just believe "in faith" that the Bible was God's Word. There were facts that set the Bible apart from any other religious writing which came before or after it. I bought a copy of Josh's book *Evidence Which Demands a Verdict,* which contained his research notes on the subject. In 2007, inspired by that book, I wrote my own study, "The Origins of the Bible." I later used it in teaching to my Sunday night discipleship training class at Pima Street Baptist Church in Tucson.

+ + + + +

In the summer of 1977, I met my wife, Stanna. I had gotten away from the psychic stuff for a while, and now with my conviction that the Bible was actually God's Word, I had started going to a college-age Bible study group at another church. On one of these Sunday nights, August 14th, I picked Stanna up and we headed for the church. On the way there we were talking, and somehow the topic of Elvis Presley came up. Stanna mentioned how he was such a generous person. And then, for no apparent reason, she said, "Can you imagine what would happen if Elvis were to die?"

Two days later when I called her after work, I had a very shaky girl on the other end of the phone. The death of Elvis was the big news story of the day, and she somehow thought that talking about it back on Sunday was connected to it actually happening. I reassured her that it was just coincidence, and that she did not make it happen.

A few days later, I went to see her, and we sat on the concrete porch in front of her parents' house. We were just casually talking, and I put my hand behind me onto the porch and started to recline, when she abruptly exclaimed, "Owwww!"

Startled, I asked her what was wrong. She replied, "You just put your hand on a sharp rock!" Feeling puzzled at her answer, I pulled my hand back out in front of me. Sure enough, a pointed piece of gravel was pressed into the lower part of my palm. *Why didn't I feel it, but she did?*

Apparently my days of dating a psychic weren't over just because I had a different girlfriend. I soon came to realize that here was a girl who could feel everything that happened to me. And she didn't have to be around me for her to feel what I felt, either. When I drove a truck for Coca-Cola® in the summer of 1981, I fell one day on a broken Coke® bottle. The jagged glass at the top of the bottle sliced through my wrist. Eight miles away, while in the swimming pool with a friend, Stanna felt it. There was nothing she could do to lessen the pain or get rid of it, but she felt the pain in my wrist, just as if it had happened to her. I have since found out that this gift is called "empathy." But back then to me it was just that "she felt everything I felt."

Empathy wasn't the only gift I discovered that Stanna has. She also has a gift for predicting death. Another gift she has is the ability to look into an animal's eyes and to know what is wrong with them. She is also psychometric as well — that is, she can hold a wrapped or covered object and get an impression of what is hidden inside. She demonstrated this gift one Christmas when I videotaped her unwrapping her presents. She would hold the package, and from either looking at it or by touching it, she would say on camera what she sensed the contents were. In all cases except for one, she was correct.

Another way she demonstrated her gift of psychometry was with "state quarters." These are coins that were issued by the U.S. government from 1999 through 2008. Each quarter had the same "heads up" design which Stanna could see and place her finger on.

But each quarter had a different design on the flip side that was unique to each of the fifty states. There was nothing on the face of the quarter itself which could give a clue as to what particular state design was on the back. Without turning the coin over, she could correctly, in every instance, describe the design on the rear of the quarter.

With artwork or paintings, she can tell what was going on with the artist at the time they created a particular work of art — what was happening in their lives, or what emotions they were feeling. Once, for example, a massage therapist we had just become acquainted with found out that Stanna was an artist, and wanted to show Stanna one of her own sketches. Upon glancing at one particular pencil-sketch of a dragon, Stanna said to her, "You were listening to the song *How Deep Is Your Love* by the Bee Gees when you drew this."

The stunned massage therapist took a few seconds to regain her composure. And then she told Stanna that indeed she had been listening to that very song. However, Stanna had her purpose behind this. The woman stayed for dinner, and while eating with us she opened up, and we found out that she was clairvoyant but was afraid to tell anyone. And this was Stanna's way to "break the ice."

+ + + + +

In the spring of 1988, I received Jesus Christ as my Lord and Savior. Although I had attended church all of my life, now I had reasons for my faith. I firmly believed that the Bible was the Word of God, and although churches aren't perfect, I believed that I needed to be part of one for proper spiritual growth. I chose the Southern Baptist church for two reasons. The first and greatest reason is that they believe that the Bible is the final word in any church teachings. Another reason I chose this church is their belief that we can read and understand the Bible for ourselves, rather than be required to accept a church leader's view of it.

The Southern Baptists' statement of faith says: "The competency of the soul in religion entails the authority of the Scriptures and the lordship of Jesus Christ. The priesthood of believers grants to every Christian the right to read and interpret the scriptures as he is led by the Holy Spirit." (Herschel H. Hobbs, *The Baptist Faith and Message* [Nashville: Convention Press, 1971], page 10). Indeed, as I became a teacher a few years later, this became the foundational reason that I was allowed to teach controversial Bible studies that didn't agree with traditional church thinking.

Have you ever read in the Bible that Jonah drowned and then God raised him to life while he was still inside the large fish? How about that the Earth does not move? Or that the Apostle Paul left his body to observe the churches he started? All of these are in the Bible, but weren't being taught in the churches. Through the Baptist faith I was able to teach these things to my class because they were supported by the Bible.

I found the Southern Baptist churches of the 1990s were far more open to people discovering their spiritual gifts, and to being empowered by the Holy Spirit to serve the Lord, than they were back in the 1970s when I was in the youth group. By 2011, I was happy to report to a friend in an email message the following:

> *The longer I teach my class, the more I have found various class members who have become used to spirit encounters and are searching for the answer to: "Why do I have this gift?" from their church and their Bible. In fact, I just found out on this past Sunday that Sonja and David both have visions, and Sonja's appear to be more mediumistic while David's are symbolic. Yet I can*

put my arms around them and say, 'Welcome! You are just like the rest of us and the Biblical characters you read about.'

+ + + + +

Even after more than thirty years of knowing psychics, I was finding that even in the mid 2000s I was still having trouble using the term "psychic," due to the connotations associated with that word. I had always associated "psychic" with people who were ostensibly in it for the money, such as those who operated psychic hotlines, or fakes who were overtly deceiving people. Stanna wasn't like any of them. She had a natural intuitive ability, which for years I would call a "sensing ability" because I couldn't picture her being in the same category as the psychics who were on radio, or in some tabloid.

There were several differences between what I saw in my wife versus those psychics, which only contributed to this disparity in my thinking. For one, she openly served the Lord and had received Jesus Christ as her Lord and Savior. I wasn't seeing any well-known psychics even talking about the Lord Jesus Christ. They might mention God or angels, but not the Lord.

Secondly, unlike those on radio or in tabloids, I never saw my wife ever try to use any divination device such as a pendulum or Tarot cards. And unlike the radio psychics I had heard, neither Stanna nor Tami ever asked anyone for their birthdate in order to know something. They "just knew" what they knew. And for many years that became the standard in my mind which I compared any psychic to.

As I became online friends with the psychics and mediums I encountered through social media, I sought understanding as to why my real life experiences with psychics weren't matching those of the psychics in the media.

Control was yet another major difference between the "psychics" and the ones I called "intuitive." With Stanna, unless a particular impression came to her mind about something, life was pretty normal. She did not read minds, and rarely predicted anything in the future unless it was someone's death — and that came as an impression that she had no control over. In contrast, the psychics I heard on radio talk shows seemed to be able to get extrasensory information at will, any time that someone asked them for a reading.

Melanie, who has been a medium her entire life, once told me that she was supposed to do a phone reading for a person in Florida. Melanie asked the person on the other end of the phone, "Is someone there named Nancy? They (the spirits) want to talk to Nancy."

Melanie's "sitter" (the living relative who requests a reading in hopes of making contact with a deceased relative), replied, "Nancy's downstairs, I'll get her." However, Nancy would not come to the phone and the reading was over. The spirit had nothing for the sitter, but for Nancy instead, who wasn't receptive to it.

Despite almost thirty-five years of knowing psychics, Melanie became the first medium who became a close friend of mine. And as I got to know her better, the Lord began showing me new things in Scripture about mediumship that I had not noticed before. One such example happened to me in church on a Sunday, approximately three weeks after first meeting her.

Before you read it, it's important to for you to know that my own spiritual gift works with the Holy Spirit for bringing Scripture to mind. Sometimes it's a rather odd Scripture — one that I wouldn't

Kevin Schoeppel

have ordinarily thought of — which makes the Spirit's role even more noticeable. As the Bible says in John 14:26 (HCSB): "The Counselor, the Holy Spirit — the Father will send Him in My name — will teach you all things and remind you of everything I have told you."

Here is what I wrote to Melanie about that experience:

> *I remembered what I wrote to you last night that the gift of mediumship is not evil, so my thought as I sat in the worship service was, 'Since Melanie's gift is NOT evil, then what would happen if she chose to serve Jesus as Lord and Savior?'*

> *One of the least expected Scriptures came to my mind: '[Jesus] was put to death in the body but made alive by the Spirit, through whom also he went and preached to the spirits in prison, who disobeyed long ago when God waited patiently in the days of Noah while the ark was being built.' (1 Peter 3:18-20)*

> *If we follow Christ, we do what he did. But we each have a part to perform in the body of Christ as he gifted us accordingly. You already know I have the gift of teaching. But who's going to communicate with disobedient spirits? Who's going to have conversations with them just like you and I do over the phone, about God's love for us and His plans for those of us who follow him?*

> *This knocks me over and gives me a view that isn't conventional for a Christian to have. But I would think that Jesus wouldn't waste His time preaching to spirits if there was no reason for Him to do so.*

But just in case I sound like a Christian that went off the deep end, consider this Bible verse too: 'For this is the reason the gospel was preached even to those who are now dead, so that they might be judged according to men in regard to the body, but live according to God in regard to the spirit.' (1 Peter 4:6)

I wouldn't have thought it! But who's been given the ability to do it? My guess is mediums are given their gift for a reason such as this.

I had finally reached the point at which I knew mediumship, like psychic ability, was a bona fide spiritual gift. But there would be more that the Spirit of the Lord would teach me about Biblical truths that He knew I had not been ready to accept previously. Since now that I was a friend to a medium, the Holy Spirit knew that my mind would be ready to understand such things. And one of these truths went contrary to a belief I had held all of my life.

This teaching of the Holy Spirit, which no person put into my mind, was so radically different from everything I had ever come to believe. But I needed to learn this teaching, because without learning it, I would not have a mind that could be open and accepting of mediumship. And I needed to be open and accepting of that in order to benefit from this spiritual gift and ultimately receive the Lord's healing.

Kevin Schoeppel

FIVE

Heaven, Hell, & the Other Side

One common belief among mediums, Christians, and those who are both, is that our lives do not end with the physical death of the body, but that our spirit continues to live on as a distinct personality. *Where* our spirits go after the death of our physical bodies is where we may disagree. Being from a Christian family, and attending and teaching in a Baptist church most of my life, I had believed that those who have received Jesus Christ as their Lord and Savior go to Heaven when they die, and those who have not go to Hell.

Mediums communicate with those "on the other side." It seems sometimes that the spirits on the other side are ever present and ready to communicate to their sitter through the mediums. Mediums don't typically speak of these crossed over spirits as being in Heaven or Hell, and usually do not indicate whether the spirit had received Jesus Christ as their Lord and Savior in their physical lifetime.

Even after becoming friends with several mediums online, I still couldn't see how they could be right about the afterlife. But I still remember praying to the Lord about how to be able to share God's love to mediums. I initially felt shortchanged, because I had to rely on the Bible for my information on the afterlife, while they were experiencing it firsthand. Whenever I prayed about this, however, I remember this thought coming back to me: *Just keep sharing my Word. My Spirit will take care of the rest.*

Before I share with you what the spirit of the Lord taught me after Melanie became part of our lives, I want to tell you what I *used* to teach on the subject of mediums and the spirits they contacted. I never bashed mediums — that is, to ever say that they were evil or got their abilities from Satan — but I still felt that the spirits that they were speaking with were misleading them and weren't really who they claimed to be.

In a lesson I wrote for my Sunday night discipleship training class several years ago, I quoted the same five verses about consulting mediums for guidance that appear at the beginning of Chapter One. And I asked the class after that, "Why does God command us not to consult mediums? Is God trying to manipulate our information sources, so that we only get our afterlife information from Him?"

To "see a ghost" implies that a person who has died is still on the Earth and can be seen, although they no longer have a physical body. For believers in Christ, I told them, there is no in-between. We are either with the Lord Jesus Christ, or we are not. *And where is that?*

Then I would quote two Scriptures, Acts 7:55-56, and Mark 16:19, to show the class that being with the Lord Jesus Christ *had to mean Heaven.* I then concluded that part of the lesson with, "Well, that was probably obvious even without the Scriptures. But it was important to establish, scripturally, that we who are redeemed by Christ are either here on Earth in the body or in Heaven with him. Period."

It seemed like a convincing argument. It was even well supported with Scripture. So how could I have possibly experienced a change of my beliefs about this?

That was from one of my written lessons. But in fact, there were several times during the years in which I taught the Sunday school and discipleship training classes that the subject of paranormal experiences, extrasensory perception, and mediumship would come up at church even when it wasn't the lesson topic. Shows like *Medium* and *Ghost Whisperer* were quite popular in the mid 2000s, and I would be asked frequently what the Bible had to say about the spirits of the dead.

When this came up, I would have the class open their Bibles us to the story of the rich man and Lazarus in Luke 16:19-31. Here it is from the *New American Standard Bible*:

> "Now there was a rich man, and he habitually dressed in purple and fine linen, joyously living in splendor every day. And a poor man named Lazarus was laid at his gate, covered with sores, and longing to be fed with the crumbs which were falling from the rich man's table; besides, even the dogs were coming and licking his sores.

> Now the poor man died and was carried away by the angels to Abraham's bosom; and the rich man also died and was buried. In Hades he lifted up his eyes, being in torment, and saw Abraham far away and Lazarus in his bosom. And he cried out and said, 'Father Abraham, have mercy on me, and send Lazarus so that he may dip the tip of his finger in water and cool off my tongue, for I am in agony in this flame.'

> But Abraham said, 'Child, remember that during your life you received your good things, and likewise Lazarus bad things; but now he is being comforted here, and you are in agony. And besides all this, between us and you there is a great chasm fixed, so that those who wish to come over from

here to you will not be able, and that none may cross over from there to us.' And he said, 'Then I beg you, father, that you send him to my father's house — for I have five brothers — in order that he may warn them, so that they will not also come to this place of torment.'

But Abraham said: 'They have Moses and the Prophets; let them hear them.' But he said, 'No, father Abraham, but if someone goes to them from the dead, they will repent!' But he said to him, 'If they do not listen to Moses and the Prophets, they will not be persuaded even if someone rises from the dead.'"

After we read this parable together, there were four things I pointed out to the students:

1. Neither the rich man nor Lazarus were presently on Earth as a spirit.

2. Neither of them could return to the Earth from where they were. If they could, then coming back to Earth would be the way to get around "the great chasm" which separated the two places.

3. When Abraham said, "They have Moses and the Prophets; let them hear them," he meant that the Scriptures they already had were sufficient to inform the rich man's brothers about life beyond the physical realm.

4. Abraham was correct when he said, "If they do not listen to Moses and the Prophets, they will not be convinced even if someone rises from the dead." In Acts 1:3 (NASB), Jesus

proved his resurrection from the dead "by many convincing proofs." Yet this has not convinced everyone to repent and turn to him as their Lord and Savior.

I followed this up with 2 Corinthians 11:14-15, and 1 John 4:1, which were my proofs to the class that mediums were indeed receiving communications from spirits — *deceiving spirits,* I told them. *With spirits who want you to believe that since their death all is fine and dandy, then who needs to follow Jesus as Lord?* The one thing I told them in defense of mediums was that most of them sincerely believed that they had brought through the spirit of the sitter's loved one, and were not aware of that spirit's deception.

Even thought I wasn't a medium-basher, keep in mind that the Holy Spirit had not yet opened my mind to what I am about to share with you now.

In November of 2010, I felt that the Holy Spirit wanted me to teach a Scriptural lesson on Heaven. So as I do with any Biblical topic, I began by doing an electronic Bible word search on the word "heaven" as a starting point to find out everything the Bible had to say about that place.

In the *New International* version of the Bible, from which I was preparing that lesson, there were 605 verses containing over 750 mentions of "heaven," "heavens," or "heavenly." Most of these verses referred to Heaven as God's dwelling, God's throne, a place above us, or described God as "the God of Heaven," or "Heavenly Father."

In the *New Testament*, Jesus used the phrase "Kingdom of Heaven." *But not one single verse in the entire Bible referred to Heaven as the place we immediately go to when we pass from this physical world.*

I looked at every single verse, and then studied them again, even though it was very time-consuming. This idea that maybe we *don't* immediately go to Heaven or Hell had shaken my beliefs so drastically that I avidly sought out other Scriptures that referred to a place beyond this physical life.

I was finding this newly dawning concept hard to accept. Could it really be that we *aren't* in Heaven immediately after we die? After several years of teaching just the opposite, I could no longer truthfully say, nor teach to my classes, that the Bible says that when we die we are in Heaven or in Hell.

2 Corinthians 5:6 and 8 (HCSB) says: "We are always confident and know that while we are at home in the body we are away from the Lord. . . and we are confident and satisfied to be out of the body and at home with the Lord."

But "with the Lord" does not necessarily mean "in Heaven." Psalm 139:7-8 (NASB) says: "Where can I go from your Spirit? Or where can I flee from your presence? If I ascend to heaven, you are there; If I make my bed in Sheol [the Hebrew name for the place of the dead], behold, you are there."

In Luke 23:43 (NASB), we are told that during the crucifixion, Jesus said to the criminal who hung on the other cross next to him: "Truly I say to you, today you shall be with Me in Paradise." But the Bible does not define *Paradise*, nor does it imply that Paradise is the same thing as Heaven.

In 2 Corinthians 12:2-4 (NASB), Paul says: "I know a man in Christ who fourteen years ago — whether in the body I do not know, or out of the body I do not know, God knows — such a man was caught up to the third heaven. And I know how such a man —

whether in the body or apart from the body I do not know, God knows — was caught up into Paradise."

Here Paul talks about this man being caught up to the "third heaven," which, interestingly, is used only in this particular verse and nowhere else in the Bible. From what Paul says here, the "third heaven" or "Paradise," seems to be a distinct and separate place from "Heaven." So this may be the place — or dimension — where persons who have had near-death or out-of-the-body experiences have been to and which they believe is actually Heaven, but is not.

For example, my stepfather, Joseph, had a near death experience. When he came back into his physical body, he recounted a beautiful place — most probably either Paradise or this "third heaven" — to which he had been transported. And he wanted to remain in this beautiful place. But he was told that he could not stay there and he reluctantly left and returned to his earthly body.

From that time until his passing in 2005, he had a living will insisting that he not be resuscitated or be put on life support. And he had notes posted around the house in case of emergency, which stated the same, as he eagerly looked forward to the day he would return to this place.

Even in the parable of the rich man and Lazarus which we just read, notice that Lazarus was not taken to Heaven, but rather to "Abraham's bosom." Abraham hadn't yet received his heavenly reward. Hebrews 11:13 (NLT) tells us: "All these people (including Abraham, named in Hebrews 11:8) died still believing what God had promised them."

Abraham later on *will be* in Heaven, for Scripture says in Luke 13:28 (KJV): "There shall be weeping and gnashing of teeth, when ye shall see Abraham, and Isaac, and Jacob, and all the prophets, in the kingdom of God, and you yourselves thrust out." *Kingdom of God* and *Kingdom of Heaven* were both used by Jesus to refer to the same place.

John 3:13 (HCSB) tells us that Jesus said to Nicodemus, a teacher of the Scriptures: "No one has ascended into heaven except the One who descended from heaven — the Son of Man." Nicodemus probably knew that the Bible said in 2 Kings 2:11 (KJV): "Elijah went up by a whirlwind into heaven." Yes, but Elijah also came down from Heaven, too — if you believe what Jesus said about John the Baptist in Matthew 11:14 (NASB): "And if you are willing to accept it, John himself is Elijah who was to come."

If no one else has been to the place we call Heaven except Jesus and Elijah, then where is everyone who has passed from this life? They are in Sheol, the Hebrew name for the place of the dead. This, in most versions of the Bible, is "the grave" or "the pit"— but is not *Hell,* despite the similar sounding of the word. Jonah 2:1 (HCSB) says: "I called to the Lord in my distress, and He answered me. I cried out for help in the belly of Sheol; You heard my voice." And again in Jonah 2:6 (HCSB): "You raised my life from the Pit, Lord my God!"

I did a word search at www.biblegateway.com, using the *Amplified Bible,* and I found that sixty-four verses in the *Old Testament* use "Sheol" as the destination for the dead. Twelve more verses in the *New Testament* use "Hades," the Greek name for the same place. If everyone were actually in Heaven or Hell immediately following their physical death, as most Christians believe, how can this statement from Jesus from John 5:28-29 (KJV), be true?:

"Marvel not at this: for the hour is coming, in the which all that are in the graves shall hear his voice, and shall come forth; they that have done good, unto the resurrection of life; and they that have done evil, unto the resurrection of damnation."

Or how could this passage from Revelation 20:12-15 (HCSB), be true as well?: "I also saw the dead, the great and the small, standing before the throne, and books were opened. Another book was opened, which is the book of life, and the dead were judged according to their works by what was written in the books. Then the sea gave up its dead, and Death and Hades gave up their dead; all were judged according to their works. Death and Hades were thrown into the lake of fire. This is the second death, the lake of fire. And anyone not found written in the book of life was thrown into the lake of fire."

The sea gave up its dead, and Death and Hades gave up their dead, but why doesn't the Bible say, "And Heaven gave up its dead?" *That is because it HAS NO DEAD,* as the only ones who have been there are Jesus and Elijah.

And who are these dead in Sheol or Hades? When I first read 1 Samuel 28:19 (NASB), it sounded very odd. The spirit of Samuel, a prophet of the Lord, says to King Saul: "The Lord will also give over Israel along with you into the hands of the Philistines therefore tomorrow you and your sons will be with me." A prophet of the Lord *and* one who disobeyed the Lord, will both be in the place of the dead?

This place isn't Heaven or Hell, because when the Bible mentioned, in Luke 13:28 (KJV) "Ye shall see Abraham, and Isaac, and Jacob, and all the prophets, in the kingdom of God," that would have to include Samuel, too. So Heaven would be *his* final destination too. But God put Saul to death for disobeying him. The Bible says in 1 Chronicles 10:13 (KJV): "Saul died for his transgression which he committed against the Lord, even against the word of the Lord, which he kept not, and also for asking counsel of one that had a familiar spirit, to enquire of it." So for both Samuel and Saul to be together in the afterlife indicates that there is something in between Heaven or Hell for all persons not alive when Jesus returns.

Colossians 1:16 (KJV) tell us that Jesus, the one by whom "were all things created, that are in heaven, and that are in earth, visible and invisible," taught in three of his parables that no one is separated in death until the end of the age and the time for judgment:

> **1st parable** – from Matthew 13:47-50 (NLT): "The Kingdom of Heaven is like a fishing net that was thrown into the water and caught fish of every kind. When the net was full, they dragged it up onto the shore, sat down, and sorted the good fish into crates, but threw the bad ones away. That is the way it will be at the end of the world. The angels will come and separate the wicked people from the righteous, throwing the wicked into the fiery furnace, where there will be weeping and gnashing of teeth."

> **2nd parable** – from Matthew 25:31-33 (NLT): "When the Son of Man comes in his glory, and all the angels with him, then he will sit upon his glorious throne. All the nations will be gathered in his presence, and he will separate the people as a shepherd separates the sheep from the goats. He will place the sheep at his right hand and the goats at his left."

> **3rd parable** – from Matthew 13:24-30 (NLT): "The Kingdom of Heaven is like a farmer who

Kevin Schoeppel

planted good seed in his field. But that night as the workers slept, his enemy came and planted weeds among the wheat, then slipped away. When the crop began to grow and produce grain, the weeds also grew. The farmer's workers went to him and said, 'Sir, the field where you planted that good seed is full of weeds! Where did they come from?'

'An enemy has done this!' the farmer exclaimed.

'Should we pull out the weeds?' they asked.

'No,' he replied, 'you'll uproot the wheat if you do. Let both grow together until the harvest. Then I will tell the harvesters to sort out the weeds, tie them into bundles, and burn them, and to put the wheat in the barn.'"

In order to understand this better, let's first look back at a confusing part of the parable of the rich man and Lazarus on pages 71 and 72. In that parable, where did the rich man go? Although the NASB Bible reads: "In Hades, he lifted up his eyes, being in torment. . ." the *King James Version* uses the word "hell." And that seems to contradict everything I have written here.

To start with, there is a translation issue. *The Scofield Reference Bible* says that the word "hell" used in Luke 16:23 was originally the Greek word "Hades," and not "the lake of fire." But this parable says that the rich man told Abraham, "I am in agony in this flame." In light of just having read the parables of the fishermen, the sheep and the goats, and the parable of the wheat and the weeds, how could this man be in Hades *and* be in agony in a fire?

I prayed and prayed on this one. I was afraid that I had no way to resolve this. The Holy Spirit kept reminding me that I hadn't resolved this conflict between what the parable of the rich man and Lazarus said, and what the other Scriptures said about the afterlife.

After reading many Scriptures containing the words "fire" and "gnashing" by doing an electronic search, the Holy Spirit showed me a parable in Matthew 22:1-14. Jesus compares the Kingdom of Heaven to a king who had prepared a wedding banquet for his son, but the invited guests made excuses and would not come. Here is the rest of that parable, from Matthew 22:8-13 (NLT):

> "And [the king] said to his servants, 'The wedding feast is ready, and the guests I invited aren't worthy of the honor. Now go out to the street corners and invite everyone you see.' So the servants brought in everyone they could find, good and bad alike, and the banquet hall was filled with guests. But when the king came in to meet the guests, he noticed a man who wasn't wearing the proper clothes for a wedding. 'Friend,' he asked, 'how is it that you are here without wedding clothes?' But the man had no reply. Then the king said to his aides, 'Bind his hands and feet and throw him into the outer darkness, where there will be weeping and gnashing of teeth.'"

First, let's understand that this parable is about refusing a generous king. Although it begins with "The kingdom of heaven is like. . ." the wedding banquet is not in Heaven, because it says that both the good *and the bad* were gathered to fill the hall with guests.

And Jesus said in Matthew 5:20 (NLT): "Unless your righteousness is better than the righteousness of the teachers of religious law and the Pharisees, you will never enter the Kingdom of Heaven." If this were Heaven, the "bad" would not be present.

Kevin Schoeppel

So this is not the wedding supper of the Lamb in Heaven mentioned in Revelation 19:7-9. Since the king's command was to "invite *everyone you see*," this would have to include people that were destitute, homeless, or simply too poor to have fine wedding clothes. And so, in order for any guest to have the appropriate wedding clothes, the king *had* to provide them, because the people were simply gathered straight off of the streets. So, of course, the man was speechless when the king questioned him about why he was not wearing the wedding clothes, because he had no excuse since the king himself furnished them.

Whenever the Bible uses symbolism, the Bible *itself* should be used first to indicate what a particular symbol means. If the Bible is God's Word, then its explanation of a symbol is the *best* explanation, and the *final word*, on what that symbol means. Any other explanation of a symbol would be based on man's association of that symbol with historical occurrences, or legends, or what he has simply been taught that the symbol means — and those explanations may differ amongst different persons or cultures.

In this case, we read in Isaiah 61:10 (NASB): "I will rejoice greatly in the Lord...for he has clothed me with garments of salvation." We can, then, rely on this verse to explain that the king represents the Lord, and the wedding garments represent the salvation he provided for the man.

So, this man — in a place where both the good and the bad have been gathered for a wedding feast — is being cast out for his refusal of the king's garments, which are his salvation. The others, once there, accepted the king's garments. For his refusal, he was cast "into the darkness, where there will be weeping and gnashing of teeth."

As you read in the parable of the fishing net, on page 78, note that this place with "weeping and gnashing of teeth," also mentions a "fiery furnace," which was not mentioned in this Parable of the Wedding Feast, but is there nonetheless.

Does it seem strange for God to offer salvation in Hades? Jesus preached to spirits (1 Peter 3:18-20), and the gospel was being preached to those who are now dead (1 Peter 4:6). Now, in addition to these other Biblical proofs that God does offer salvation there, in Matthew 16:18 (NASB) Jesus tells Peter: "I will build My church; and the gates of Hades will not overpower it." Why would Jesus say that the church would even come to the gates of Hades? To bring the message of salvation — which is clearly what the other two verses are saying. And just who in the church would be able to contact anyone in Hades to bring salvation? That's right. . .*mediums!*

Many Christians mistakenly believe that once they have received Christ as their Lord and Savior, they do not face judgment but go right into Heaven upon death, and that this judgment is for those who do not have Christ as Lord and Savior. But this is NOT what the Bible says. In 2 Corinthians 5:9-10 (NLT), we read: "So whether we are here in this body or away from this body, our goal is to please him. For we must all stand before Christ to be judged. We will each receive whatever we deserve for the good or evil we have done in this earthly body."

And if we all must appear at the judgment, we couldn't be in Heaven before the judgment, since Heaven would have no dead to give up within it.

Not only does this passage say that we ALL must appear at that judgment, but that we must still make it our goal to please Christ when we are *not* in our physical bodies *because of that judgment.*

And the passage implies that we have work to do when we are outside of our bodies, too!

I once asked Melanie what people who were not in their bodies any longer were doing. "We continue to study when we are on the other side," she told me. "We still desire to know more about the Lord and his ways. And even though we died, we still have the same interests as when we were on Earth. We ask ourselves how we could have better lived our lives."

Mediums such as Melanie have come closer to the real truth than many Christians, but have not previously been able to acknowledge it — by a Biblical standard, that is.

The Bible discusses Heaven and Hell far more than Hades, which precedes judgment, because God is far more interested in our final destinies and what we do now to secure them. "Now is the acceptable time; now is the day of salvation," says 2 Corinthians 6:2 (HCSB).

Although the evidence is in the Bible of the gospel being preached to spirits, the Bible commands that *now*, in this life, is the time to begin serving the Lord. In Philippians 1:21-24, we are told that to be serving Christ Jesus *now,* while still in the body, is a benefit to others and a reward to the one serving. That Scripture tells us that we receive rewards for things done while in the body.

Scripture tells us as well of a "second death." As we read earlier from Revelation 20:14 (HCSB): "Death and Hades were thrown into the lake of fire. This is the second death, the lake of fire."

The Bible also says in Revelation 21:7-8 (NASB): "He who overcomes (has Jesus as their Lord and Savior) will inherit these things, and I will be his God and he will be My son. But for the cowardly and unbelieving and abominable and murderers and immoral persons and sorcerers and idolaters and all liars, their part will be in the lake that burns with fire and brimstone, which is the second death."

Since the spirit realm (Hades, or Sheol) will be thrown into that "second death," *it is very important, if you have not already done so, that you receive Christ as your Lord and Savior to not be in that second death.*

Just as I am not able to see beyond this physical life, I believe that mediums are limited to seeing the realm of "the other side." Some may have been to the "third heaven" or "paradise," and reported what they have seen there. But those visions are not Heaven either, because the thief crucified next to Jesus has also been to "paradise."

Although in Revelation the apostle John was shown Heaven, he did not see what the Lord has prepared there for those of us who love him. (1 Corinthians 2:9) And our minds have not imagined what that is either. The reason, I believe, that God does not reveal what he has prepared is because he wants us to trust his word about what he says he will do.

Imagine that you have a beautiful home prepared for you and ready for you to move into, but it's on the other side of the country from where you currently reside. You load up your belongings and make the journey to your new home. On the way, you need to stop at a hotel for the night. You do so and you make a call to a friend back home. You haven't seen your new home yet, but you tell your friend how this hotel has a swimming pool, a sauna, a workout room, and even serves a continental breakfast.

The friend tells other friends of yours whom you left behind about how you spoke to him from this great hotel you are in. But is this as far as you are going? Are you going to spend the rest of your

Kevin Schoeppel

life in the hotel, or are you on your way to your true destination — the beautiful home which has been prepared for you?

A medium would be like your friend on the other end of the phone. He has made contact with you in your temporary dwelling — such as the "other side" — but as yet, he hasn't heard from you from your eternal home, because you are not there yet.

The Bible does speak of Christ's return, judgment, and Heaven or Hell, of which I do not normally hear mediums speak. I do firmly believe it was the Holy Spirit alone who taught me that we first arrive in Sheol upon our physical deaths. This did not come from a sermon in any church. Nor did I have a Bible study book to follow which suggested any of this teaching. It was just me alone in my study, with just the Holy Spirit and an electronic Bible on my computer.

The Spirit had his purpose for it, though. My mind was now fully receptive to benefit from the gift of mediumship, without the reservations and previous beliefs I carried that there was no way our loved ones could be contacting us through a medium. But now the Spirit had taught me differently using God's Word. And so I was prepared for a healing experience.

SIX

A Medium Comes Through For Me

The Lord may have a special calling for all those with psychic gifts. A psychic or medium can make a true and positive difference in a person's life, and can sometimes break through years of mental strongholds where churches and pastors cannot or have failed. It is my hope that all mediums whom the Spirit has chosen to receive this special gift will see just how important their work can be in turning someone around both mentally and spiritually. Here is my personal experience of how a medium came through for me:

My stepmother in Kansas left an urgent message on my answering machine the night of August 4, 1992. I called her back immediately only to find that my dad had passed away at 8:30 P.M. that evening. I didn't have the money to travel there for the funeral, so she bought my round-trip ticket so I could attend. I didn't get emotional. I just wasn't that way over deaths, even if it was my own father or mother.

The part that hit me the hardest was when I received a copy of my father's will a few months later. He had willed his possessions to my stepmother, which is what I had expected that he would do. The part that really upset me was the provision in his will that dealt with the distribution of his estate in the event of my stepmother's death. He had requested that his estate be divided up between my stepsister and my stepbrother.

In particular, what upset me was these words he had written: "I am not unmindful that I have a son, Kevin John, and he is specifically excluded from this will."

Kevin Schoeppel

To me I wasn't disinherited — *I was disowned*. And I could not figure out why. I wasn't the "black sheep" of the family. I had not cheated him, disrespected him, or taken advantage of him. I was not a criminal, a thief, a con artist, draft dodger, drug dealer, or any other disreputable sort of person. I was not lazy, begging, bumming off of others, borrowing without repaying, or on welfare.

At the time I could only come up with two reasons that he did this. It was either that I had not been able to give him grandchildren (at the time of his death my son Ryan was not born yet), or that I was not financially successful to his satisfaction. When I asked my stepmother about this later, she said that he had stated to her that he did not want grandchildren from me anyway if they came from Stanna. This caused my wife to shed many tears, wondering what she had ever done to him to make him say such a cruel thing.

Obviously now I couldn't confront my dad. He was dead. All I could do was speculate. And for the next several years, I did just that — wonder what it was about me that made him disinherit/disown me. For many years afterward, whenever the subject of my being disinherited by my father came up in conversation, I felt compelled to make sure that the other person understood that the money wasn't what I was upset about. My stepmother was in good health and it was very unlikely that she was going to die and not inherit his estate. I saw that provision in his will as his way of really letting me know that he had rejected me as his son. And of course it made me angry at him, wondering what expectation he had of me that I had failed to live up to.

I knew that in Exodus 20:12 (KJV), God's Word said: "Honor thy father and thy mother: that thy days may be long upon the land which the Lord thy God giveth thee." So I could not bad-mouth him and his action toward me, no matter how I felt. I could only keep it to myself and try to not think about it.

However, as I tried, I found that this sad ending to my relationship with my father could not be put to rest as it should have been. Quite to the contrary, since I went to church regularly, I now had to deal with some very ugly spiritual issues on top of being disowned.

The first of these happened two years later when the pastor of our church decided to teach a Bible study on blessings, which centered on the story of Jacob and Esau found in the 27th chapter of Genesis in the Bible. For those who are unfamiliar with it, Esau and Jacob were brothers and their father, Isaac, before he passes away, was supposed to bless Esau, the oldest brother. But Jacob disguised himself as Esau by putting on his brother's clothing and by putting goatskins on his arms so that they felt hairy like Esau's. Isaac was blind at that time, and therefore was fooled into thinking that Jacob was really Esau. So Isaac ended up giving Jacob the blessing intended for Esau.

While I was still trying to cope with being disinherited by my dad, this story of Jacob and Esau caused me to consider a much more serious question: *What is so important about receiving a father's blessing that Jacob was willing to lie to his father and deceive him to get it?*

In the study, I asked my pastor that question. But the pastor could not — or maybe, *would not* — answer my question. So I formed my own conclusion: *God goes along with whatever your father wanted for you.* If your dad blessed you, God blessed you. And if your dad rejected you, God rejected you. Or maybe you were cursed. Rejection of the blessing was a major problem for big brother Esau too, because the *New Testament* makes reference to it in Hebrews 12:17 (NLT): "When [Esau] wanted his father's blessing, he was rejected. It was too late for repentance, even though he begged with bitter tears."

No normal person wants to believe that God has rejected them. But after my dad rejected me, and having formed my own conclusion from the story of Jacob and Esau, I began looking for any sign that might tell me if God had rejected me or not. One such "sign" came later that same year in a different Bible study at our church. During that Bible study this verse, John 8:47 (KJV), was brought up: "He that is of God heareth God's words: ye therefore hear them not, because ye are not of God."

Since I had often heard other Christians say that God had spoken to them, or that God wanted them to do this or that, I would at times wonder why God would not speak to me the way he must speak to them — and now I "knew" why: *I must not be of God.* So I vehemently threw the study book in the trash and walked out of the Bible study.

A year later, before my son, Ryan, had been born I was listening to a Christian radio program in which they were discussing Psalm 127:3 (NLT): "Children are a gift from the Lord; they are a reward from him." The host of the program had the nerve to comment, "Wouldn't you agree that the opposite is also true, that having no children is a curse from the Lord?" I became so bitterly angry at this host's blunt comment that I snapped off the radio so hard I almost broke the volume knob.

During that time there were other things that would hit my heart the wrong way too. "A wise son makes a father glad," says Proverbs 15:20 (NASB). *Did this mean that I was a fool?*

+ + + + +

Almost two years after I had walked out of the Bible study, my belief that God had rejected me had so adversely affected my thoughts and actions to the point that Stanna told me I should get some counseling. "We're supposed to *give* the help, not get it," I flatly told her.

"But you're teaching children at the church," she replied. "And you can't keep having these angry feelings about your father. Kids will see right through you." And so she finally broke through and convinced me to at least ask the pastor at our church about getting some counseling.

Even after I admitted that I needed the counseling, getting up the courage to ask for help was another challenge for me. When I finally was ready, I stayed around late at the church one Wednesday evening until only the pastor and I were left. "I think I might need some counseling," I told him. "Do you know where I could get some that won't be expensive?"

"Remind me of that on Sunday" he said, stating that he needed to get home. So I did just as he had asked me to on the next Sunday — waited around to remind him. He saw me, went for his car, and quickly drove off. I was now very puzzled.

A few weeks passed. I was having coffee with a friend of mine, a seminary student who knew our pastor well, and I told him what had happened. "That's one of the tactics he uses when he really doesn't want to talk to someone," he said. "He told me once that someday when I become a pastor and if I don't want to deal with someone, just tell that person to remind you of whatever it is on Sunday. He said that then you can see them coming and get away."

I was furious now — not with my friend, but with the pastor. I tried to be understanding about it and look at the situation from the pastor's point of view. Maybe our pastor really was just too busy

Kevin Schoeppel

for me. Or did he feel I was a "problem person?" After hearing what my friend had said to me, I felt now like I had not only been rejected by my dad, *and* by God, *but by my pastor as well.* I still had been secretly hoping, deep down inside, that maybe I had somehow misunderstood the Bible — and that I would find out that I wasn't really cursed or rejected by God.

Stanna and I continued to teach our class of kids at the church throughout the summer of 1997. But every time I heard our pastor talk about visiting with another church member, I became very bitter. I would think: *What did they have to do to get him to spend time with them? Slip him a $20 bill?* Actually, at this point I had come to believe that he didn't feel I was worth spending any time on — but other church members *were* worth his time. What did others have that I didn't?

The more I heard, the angrier I got. On August 3, 1997, I reached the end of my patience and left that church. And on August 25, 1997, we discovered that Stanna was pregnant.

We visited a new church about a mile away from the one we left, and that church's pastor wanted to visit us and invited us to come back. We agreed to meet with him, and I finally had my chance to ask my questions to another pastor. "You know the story of Jacob and Esau — you know, how Jacob tricks his father, Isaac, into giving him his brother's blessing? Well, my father disinherited me, and if my father is displeased with me, does that mean God is displeased with me too?"

The pastor explained that in the *New Testament* in Matthew 10:37 (NLT), Jesus had said: "If you love your father or mother more than you love me, you are not worthy of being mine." And he went on to explain that in some cases, Jesus' command might not have pleased that person's father. One such instance from Matthew

4:21-22 (NLT), tells us that "[Jesus] saw two other brothers, James and John, sitting in a boat with their father, Zebedee, repairing their nets. And he called them to come, too. They immediately followed him, leaving the boat and their father behind."

The pastor pointed out that Zebedee probably was upset with his sons for doing such a thing. But, the pastor assured me, that whether the father, Issac, blessed Jacob or not, the Lord had already said in Genesis 25:23 (NLT): "Your older son will serve your younger son," referring to Jacob and Esau before either boy was born. While I still had no clue as to why I was disinherited, this new pastor had at least given me the answer I had been hoping for. God really had not rejected me. Feeling completely accepted by God was more of a gradual process, but I felt more confident to teach since I now was certain that I did belong to the Lord.

On March 31, 1998, our first child, a boy, was born. I made a promise to myself that now that I was a father, I would never do what my own father had done. I would always be a part of his life. Ryan would inherit everything I owned, and I would never do anything to change that. I would always let him know I was proud of him. And if he ever did anything wrong, I would make sure he knew what he was being corrected for so that he would never have to be left wondering what he did.

In 1999, I began to teach an adult Sunday school class at our new church. Now with the knowledge that God was not rejecting me just because my father had, I was able to just bury the thought of my father — until something would remind me of him. Then I would have to make myself forget him again and move on. I didn't want to think about him anymore. Thoughts of him still only caused me depression and anger. I simply had to live with that rejection the best way I knew how — push it away and forget it.

+ + + + +

Several years went by and social media networks began to form on the Internet. I opened an account on one of them and soon became acquainted with Tania, a medium in London, Ontario, Canada. Although I had never asked any medium for readings, I often asked her questions on the abilities of a medium. In one discussion with her, she mentioned that the London Spiritualist Church met in a building owned by the Masonic Lodge of London. My dad had been a Master Mason, and so I brought the subject of him up to her in an email:

> *I admit that when it comes to my dad, I'm angry with the Masons. While my dad always did have a temper, he was always a very practical person, and although many times he was controlling, he wasn't a person to ostracize family members from one another until he became involved with the Masons. I was disinherited mainly, I believe, because I would not join them. But to me it was like saying, 'If you are going to turn your back on the Masons, you've turned your back on me.'*

> *Grrr. I look back now, as a dad myself, and remember how I loved my dad and he took me to ballgames the same way I took Ryan recently — before those Masons intervened. I only care to remember him the way he was BEFORE then.*

> *Sorry, I'm getting worked up as I write this. Of course you know that in serving the Lord I don't ask for readings, but I thought to myself once that even if the Lord said, 'Yes,' what would I really want to hear? Would I really want to hear more criticism from someone on the other side about what a disappointment my life is to them? You said once that the first rule is that a spirit can't*

physically hurt us. The words are another thing, Tania.

Maybe this has happened to you that a client left hurt and then shunned mediums? It wouldn't be your fault, of course, but the client maybe just wasn't prepared for a barrage of disdain when the spirit came through. After all, you can only give what's given.

Would you have spared the feelings of a client and claimed they didn't come through in such a case? Or do you say, 'He did come through, but I don't want to hurt you?' Strange, I never thought I'd be asking this.

Tania wrote back to me:

Hi Kevin. First rule of mediumship: Accept no negative energies to present. Second rule: If one does come forward, thank them and send them packing. I NEVER receive messages that are anything but apologetic from those in spirit. I have read for a great many people who have lived a life of pain due to a parent or significant other. When and if that person presents himself or herself, I always tell the sitter, 'I have so and so here. Are you comfortable with this, and would you like to receive their message?'

It is very common to have spirit come in for the strict reason of saying; 'I am so sorry.' I get a lot of tears from the sitter most times. Just sitting here trying to make this connection with your dad, I am compelled to tell you that much of your dad's decision to become part of such a clandestine group of men was simply the need to be accepted. It does not condone what he did, and does not condone the belief system that prevailed, but there it is. It is difficult at times for a child to understand that a parent can possibly have an issue with self-esteem or ego. Yet there it is — the root of people's actions.

You say that in serving the Lord you do not ask for readings. How accepting would you be if, by chance, I just woke up one day and thought, 'Wow I have this message to pass along to Kevin.' Would that be acceptable? I do feel that if I was permitted to bring your dad into my energy that you might be quite surprised at what he truly does feel. Simply right now by thinking of him I have him drawing in. Spirits who are malicious or angry will not do this. . .that is very telling to me. You let me know. And keep smiling Kevin. You are a good person.

This should have brought closure, but it did not then. And it wasn't Tania's fault. I still had that mistaken belief at the time that those who had Jesus Christ as their Lord and Savior were in Heaven and those who did not were in Hell. And so any spirit who appeared to mediums then must be an impostor sent to fool both the medium and the sitter. I really hadn't applied the Biblical test to determine this. *It was a logical conclusion based on a mistaken belief.* This is the reason why I said that I needed to learn that, upon our deaths, we aren't immediately in Heaven or Hell. As you see, this mistaken belief I still carried at that time interfered with my mental acceptance of Tania's message. Mediumship could be of no value to me yet.

I can still remember re-reading Tania's response on Father's Day, just a few weeks later, thinking to myself how it would have been so nice "if only" that spirit that came through to her really was my dad wanting to make amends instead of a "deceiving spirit." As you know, I had more to learn.

Still, Tania had presented a question to me in that message that would become very important to my future relationship with any psychic or medium. Her question was: *If she had a message that she felt she needed to pass on to me, would I be accepting of that message?* To that question, this is what I replied:

> *You asked me the question of whether I would be open to you feeling compelled to pass on to me something you received. Yes, I am always open to such messages. I have always taken seriously any impressions Stanna may have had. The Scriptural commands always referred to me not being permitted to "turn to" mediums.*
>
> *However, part of the reason I didn't expect the answer I got is because of your calling or profession in this area. As a professional medium, I would not have expected you to do free readings, nor would I have tried to 'sneak one in.' You make your living that way, and I respect that.*
>
> *But on the flip side of the coin, if anyone feels that there is something that won't rest until the message is passed on to me, that there is an urgency that I receive their message, there is no way I can turn that down. For all I know, I might be shutting out a message from the Lord to me, whether Stanna, Ryan, a friend, or a medium is the messenger.*

Little did I know then, as I was writing that reply to Tania, that I was just beginning the "renewing of the mind" process — spoken of in Romans 12:2 — which would lead me to a closer friendship with a medium, which in turn would allow the Holy Spirit to reveal Biblical truths to me as I was ready to receive them.

Just a little more than a year after that time, Melanie contacted Tania to find a channeling teacher, since there was no one who taught such in her geographic area. When Melanie first contacted me, I was puzzled at what she wanted, and even more puzzled that Tania responded by referring her to me. I contacted Melanie briefly and I told her I was sorry, that I didn't do that — teach channeling — and that I was a Christian who taught the Bible, but was married to a psychic. She couldn't understand either what caused Tania to refer her to me, but I told her maybe she was supposed to be taught directly by Spirit, which is in 1 John 2:27.

After that we talked again, and she couldn't get enough of asking me questions on the Bible and spiritual gifts. It seems as though members of her family, who supposedly were Christians, had been bashing her all of her life for having her gifts. She even told me that one of them had said that in the Bible, women didn't prophesy. I told her, "Apparently they didn't read Joel 2:28 (KJV), which says: 'I will pour out my spirit upon all flesh; and your sons *and your daughters* shall prophesy.'"

I never would have thought it — a medium wanting to learn the Bible from me? We had several more phone calls and I answered a lot of her questions on spiritual gifts. Her abilities, according to her, became stronger as a result.

I thanked Tania for bringing Melanie and me together, and she replied:

So glad that you have all made such a wonderful connection. I simply go with my gut when putting energies together. It will do Melanie so much good and you will all learn something from one another. I see a lifelong friendship developing here. Good for Stanna too. . .her senses seem to be shifting into high gear as of late. That is awesome.

Melanie and I continued to be friends just as Tania predicted. I knew Melanie used a video calling program to call her grandson, so I downloaded it myself to try it out and I called her. We had a few problems getting started, but finally got connected. I swiveled my office chair and positioned the camera so that she would see the "good side" of my office, and not the clutter. Immediately behind me in her view, was a bookcase with an antique radio on top of it.

The first thing she said to me was: "Your dad is glad to see that you still have that radio that he gave you."

I replied simply, "He gave that radio to me when I was eleven years old. It still works but I don't play it much." Often, in the moment, the implications of what I'm hearing just don't sink in until later. Three days passed when I suddenly realized that *I had never previously told Melanie about any object in my office*, or how it had been acquired. And so she *must* have actually gotten that information from my dad! Upon that realization, I wrote her an email:

Oh, Melanie . . .about the radio. The one thing that I still have an embarrassment about was when you said my dad was here Monday night. No, YOU did not embarrass me. Just for once I was GLAD that I do not hear spirits, as I never seemed to please my dad at anything. I know that our house *is cluttered. I remember how he was upset that we didn't maintain a neat home and he blamed it all on Stanna and said that she was ruining my life. I've just had some angry feelings over the last day or so about him. I only had $15.43 in the bank and spent $12.18 of that for food today. I think he hates me for failure to have enough money. Stanna never complains. She helps. She always makes me feel better.*

What did I ever do him? My dad disinherited me. And it's not the money I miss. The first line of inheritance was to my stepmother, which I'm fine with. I wouldn't have received a cent in the normal manner anyway. He just had to make sure I got the message clearly that he was disowning me.

I don't steal, I never cheated anyone, I don't go back on my word, I've never abused my wife or son, I've never asked to borrow their money. I'm not a criminal nor have I ever gone to jail. So what's the point of my dad hanging around now? Is he going to get to Stanna and Ryan, since I'm the non-medium? I wish I could just cast him out and make him leave my family alone! I'm sorry. . .

In her reply message to me the next day, she wrote:

I feel that his drawing me to the radio was more of a 'knowing.' He knows now what he did to you and has gone past that.

That afternoon I talked to Melanie again on the phone. "Kevin," she said, "your dad wasn't there to criticize you. He wanted me to let you know you *outdid* him."

"*Outdid* him? How? I never made as much money as he did, and I don't have a fine home the way he did. How could I outdo him?"

"Kevin, those things aren't really important on the other side," she explained. "He's had time to learn what is important. It's relationships. He's seen how you've stayed married to your wife, and how you've been there for your son, and that you've taken care of them. He wanted me to let you know he's proud of you."

I was driving on the freeway listening to this on my cell phone. Suddenly I felt big, salty tears welling up in my eyes, and I started to choke up. Trying to get out the words best as I could, I told Melanie, "I've waited twenty years to hear this. Since he's dead, I thought I'd never hear it."

"He thinks you're a good man, Kevin."

My reply was garbled as I disconnected the call. That evening, I emailed Melanie again:

> *You have no idea how much you opened my heart up with a message I wished I could have heard from my dad for the last twenty years. To tell me he was sorry and that I outdid him — I was so stunned and overwhelmed with — well, what do you call it?*
>
> *It meant so much to hear for once from his view that I was doing good just to be who I am. It is important to know that if the money wasn't the standard, nor status, or successful position, but to take care of my wife and son and have a home for them and working hard to provide, NOW means that I 'outdid him.' I'll remember this for the rest of my life, Melanie. I spent twenty years 'paying*

Kevin Schoeppel

for failing' the first fourteen years of my adult life in his eyes. I've never emailed or called someone on the other side. . .I don't think I could call this a reading but if you see him, here goes:

Dear Dad: You have no idea how good you made me feel after what you told Melanie. I admit my eyes are watering and I can't see the keyboard well, but I love you for being proud of how I have taken care of my family. I'm glad I'm not disowned and I accept your apology. It was kind of like getting a letter from you like when you were stationed in France, or at Barksdale, or in Thailand, just through a medium this time and not the postal service.

I used to love getting those letters from you when I was little and I know there was twice I had said when you were alive, and after I got married, that if you couldn't accept me for who I was, to forget you had a son. I felt that when you disinherited me that was the final rejection and there was nothing I could do, nothing would ever change, and that I had to live with it.

I just wanted you to know now, by way of Melanie, that I really appreciate you giving her the message that you did. It meant so much and I told her I will treasure that message from now and for the rest of my life. You might have been here all along, but without her abilities I couldn't give you a hug like you've probably seen me do in all those years. Maybe she will do it for me if you come to her.

I had to wipe tears away and I'm doing it again. I'm spending the day with Ryan tomorrow, I need to make a trip to Nogales for some medicine and we'll do some other things. I'm so proud of you for what you said. I know that tomorrow I'll think of when we went to Houston in your brand new '69 Chevy, just you and I. And we went to the Astrodome, the Manned Spacecraft Center, and out to Galveston, and I won't have that cloud of "I wish it hadn't gone bad" feeling that I have had for over twenty years anymore. I have no idea how it all works on that side, just hope you get this from Melanie. I love you. ~ Kevin.

That was February 23, 2012. After six months had gone by, one day I suddenly realized that a thought which used to make me angry on a daily basis now hadn't come to my mind for several months. Without going into any great detail, I thought about it for a while. And then I realized just how many of my previous mental hang-ups about work, family relationships, acceptance by friends, and being able to make an adequate living, had also vanished from my mind.

Somehow now, it seemed that, no matter how matter how much or how little I earned, knowing that my dad was proud of me for the job I was doing taking care of my family had made a lot of my other frustrations with life disappear. I still don't understand why a message from my dad would do this, because it seemed that so many of those problems really had nothing to do with my dad. But they must have been connected somehow in my mind, for so many of them to be resolved in this way. I can't say that *all* of my problems or mental hang-ups were over, but a lot of them were.

What Melanie had done for me with her gift was something that God meant for her to do. We learn from Matthew 7:16-18 (HCSB), that Jesus said: "You'll recognize them by their fruit. Are grapes

Kevin Schoeppel

gathered from thorn bushes, or figs from thistles? In the same way, every good tree produces good fruit, but a bad tree produces bad fruit. A good tree can't produce bad fruit; neither can a bad tree produce good fruit." The manifested "fruit" of Melanie's mediumistic ability was my mind being healed. This was far beyond what anyone else had been able to do for me for twenty years.

The pastors and the churches were able to do some good by assuring me that God had not rejected me. But their abilities were inadequate to bring about a more complete mental and spiritual healing. Why? By rejecting mediums, the church is missing one of the gifts of the Spirit that it desperately needs to build up its members, and to serve the Lord as they were meant to. Just as a mechanic cannot do his job properly without the right tools, neither can the church do its job of building up its people spiritually if one of the tools needed to do the job properly is missing — in this case, mediumship. James 1:17 (KJV) says: "Every good gift and every perfect gift is from above, and cometh down from the Father of lights, with whom is no variableness, neither shadow of turning."

It was necessary for me to tell you all of this, because as you read on into the next two chapters, where we discuss Biblically the purpose and roles of the different spiritual gifts, you will be able to recall this story and know with a certainty that mediumship, when used in a way that glorifies God, *does* "build up" people and prepare them to serve him.

SEVEN
What Are the Various Spiritual Gifts
& What is Their Purpose?

Jesus commanded us to wait for the Spirit's power before doing any work for Him. He said to his disciples in Luke 24:49 (NLT): "I will send the Holy Spirit, just as my Father promised. But stay here in the city until the Holy Spirit comes and fills you with power from heaven." And later on — just before he ascends to Heaven — he tells them: "You will receive power when the Holy Spirit has come upon you; and you shall be my witnesses both in Jerusalem, and in all Judea and Samaria, and even to the remotest part of the earth." (Acts 1:8, NASB)

Jesus commanded us to wait for the Spirit's power because we really can't serve Him unless we are empowered by the Spirit. We can try. But any efforts that are of our own power will wind up being a waste of time — and possibly cause people we meet to shun Christ instead of wanting to serve Him. Isaiah 64:6 (KJV) says: "All our righteousnesses are as filthy rags." Jesus' command to his disciples as we read in John 15:4-5 (NLT) was: "Remain in me, and I will remain in you, for a branch cannot produce fruit if it is severed from the vine, and you cannot be fruitful unless you remain in me. Yes, I am the vine; you are the branches. Those who remain in me, and I in them, will produce much fruit. For apart from me you can do nothing"

You don't have to look far to see examples of people claiming to serve Jesus Christ and yet who are accomplishing nothing. How many times have you met a Christian you felt uncomfortable being around? You don't feel drawn to them. You don't feel that they have something in their lives that you wish you had too. You just wish they would go away and leave you alone.

Jesus was so much the opposite of these kinds of people. Everyone wanted to come to see Him! Mark 1:45 (NLT) says: "Large crowds soon surrounded Jesus, and he couldn't publicly enter a town anywhere. He had to stay out in the secluded places, but people from everywhere kept coming to him." This is just one of many times in the Bible that we read of crowds of people following Jesus. He had something that they wanted. And if we remain in Jesus, and He remains in us, there will be people who want something that we have in our lives too, instead of being one of those persons that people shy away from.

Having the Holy Spirit in our lives is our way of remaining in Jesus so that we have the ability to serve Him. In the following Scripture passage (John 14:15-20, NLT), Jesus says that *the Spirit* will be in us, and in the next sentence Jesus himself says that *He* will be in us: "If you love me, obey my commandments. And I will ask the Father, and he will give you another Advocate, who will never leave you. He is the Holy Spirit, who leads into all truth. The world cannot receive him, because it isn't looking for him and doesn't recognize him. But you know him, because he lives with you now and later will be in you. No, I will not abandon you as orphans — I will come to you. Soon the world will no longer see me, but you will see me. Since I live, you also will live. When I am raised to life again, you will know that I am in my Father, and you are in me, and I am in you."

It is important for you to know what different kinds of spiritual gifts that there are, because many persons are not aware of all of them. Not knowing about all of the possible spiritual gifts could lead many people to believe that they are not spiritually gifted. And then they would focus on trying to attain a gift that they really weren't given by the Holy Spirit, because they were never aware of the gift that he *did* give them.

Here is a list of thirty-one spiritual gifts that are specifically listed in the Bible, but there are more. First, between the three lists of spiritual gifts in the *New Testament* (found in 1 Corinthians 12:7-10 and 28, Romans 12:6-8, and Ephesians 4:11-13), we have:

1. Message of wisdom
2. Message of knowledge (which we may call psychic, since we obtain the knowledge supernaturally)
3. Faith
4. Healing
5. Miraculous powers
6. Prophecy
7. Distinguishing between spirits
8. Speaking in different kinds of tongues
9. Interpretation of tongues
10. Apostleship
11. Pastoring
12. Teaching
13. Ability to help others
14. Administration
15. Encouraging
16. Contributing to the needs of others
17. Leadership
18. Mercy
19. Evangelism

Then in the *Old Testament* we find:

20. Artistic craftsmanship (Exodus 35:30-35)
21. Justice (Isaiah 28:5-6)
22. Strength (Judges 14:5-6)

Kevin Schoeppel

23. Revealing of mysteries (Daniel 2:27-28)
24. Interpretation of dreams (Genesis 41:15-16)
25. Music (2 Samual 23:1)
26. Speech (2 Samual 23:2)
27. Rest (Isaiah 63:13)
28. Guidance (Isaiah 63:14)
29. Boldness (Micah 3:8)
30. Ability to see the unseen (2 Kings 6:15-17)
31. Ability to enjoy your work (Ecclesiastes 5:19)

I say that there are more, because as we are told in John 14:12 (NLT), Jesus said to his followers: "I tell you the truth, anyone who believes in me will do the same works I have done, and even greater works, because I am going to be with the Father." Some of the things that Jesus had done included knowing thoughts, predicting the future, casting out demons, healing the sick, and raising the dead. "The same works I have done," would include *anything* Jesus had done in his ministry, including those aforementioned abilities.

For example, mediumship is not specifically listed as a spiritual gift by any one verse. But if we turn to 1 Peter 3:18-19 (NLT), we read: "Christ suffered for our sins once for all time. . . He suffered physical death, but he was raised to life in the Spirit. So he went and preached to the spirits in prison." Well, if Jesus preached to spirits — and he said that "anyone who believes in me will do the same works I have done," — then that would mean that there will be people who are gifted with the ability to communicate with spirits too, by the power of the Spirit.

Out of the list of the thirty-one gifts I have listed, there are only about ten of them which really appear to be supernatural to an observer — that is, they look like something that you could not possibly do without being empowered by God. Among these are knowledge, healing, miraculous powers, interpretation of dreams, and prophecy. Because of the more obvious supernatural nature of these gifts, it's easy to think these are the greater gifts of the Spirit.

My gift is one of the gifts of the Spirit which does not appear to be supernatural to a casual observer. "Teaching?" you say. "So what? Anyone can learn to be a teacher." But those who are given this gift by the Spirit know that their own natural ability cannot produce the results they see. And those who benefit from a gifted teacher can tell the difference.

At the end of Jesus' Sermon on the Mount, we read in Matthew 7:28-29 (NLT) : "When Jesus had finished saying these things, the crowds were amazed at his teaching, for he taught with real authority — quite unlike their teachers of religious law."

An elderly couple once told me, "We've gone to Sunday school all of our lives, and we heard the same old things over and over again. But in your class, Kevin, we actually learn something." What made the difference? *The power of the Spirit!*

The gift "contributing to the needs of others," doesn't look like a spiritual gift at all, until you try to do it on your own without the Spirit. 2 Corinthians 9:9-15 explains the details of this gift. God multiplies all of our efforts for the purpose of giving. We all know how difficult it is for the average person to accumulate wealth. So imagine a person with this gift (1) receiving more assets than he knows how to accumulate, then (2) having the power to resist taking some of this for himself, and then (3) having the wisdom and knowledge to distribute it all to people really in need, without being scammed or being taken advantage of in the process.

Although nothing looks supernatural about one who has this gift — we don't see the dead coming to life, a lame man jumping up and walking, or someone knowing something psychically — we have to admit that for anyone to be able do even *one* of the three tasks of this gift requires supernatural ability.

So for those that have one of the many non-supernatural appearing gifts, it is important to understand that we often can't see that we have the gift that the Spirit has given to us until other people notice it and tell us. With my gift as a teacher, I have often been told by people that they had prayed to the Lord many times for the answer to a question they had about the Bible — and that I gave them their answer without ever knowing anything about the question.

One year during the Christmas season, a woman who had taught a women's Bible study at our church for more than forty years, until she moved away, came to my Sunday school class while visiting Tucson. As sometimes happened, we would deviate off of the topic of the lesson, and I would answer questions that the people in the class had on their minds about the Bible. After class, this woman asked me, "How do you do it? I could never do what I see you doing!" I just told her that the Holy Spirit was the teacher, and I could only do what I did because of Him.

Everyone who has truly chosen to follow Christ has the Holy Spirit, and therefore has at least one gift of the Holy Spirit. Peter said in Acts 2:38-39 (HCSB): "Repent," Peter said to them, "and be baptized, each of you, in the name of Jesus Christ for the forgiveness of your sins, and you will receive the gift of the Holy Spirit. For the promise is for you and for your children, and for all who are far off, as many as the Lord our God will call."

Sometimes it's difficult for a person to recognize that they have a spiritual gift if it doesn't appear to be a supernatural gift. If you were to ask me, "When did you realize that you had the spiritual gift of teaching?" I couldn't give you a definite answer. Because I would hear just as often my gift put into the context of natural ability as in, "You sure seem to know your Bible" or "You sure have a good memory." It's one thing for others to recognize that you are gifted and for them to tell you so, and quite another thing for you to *believe* you are actually spiritually gifted when you know you aren't a psychic, medium, healer, or miracle worker.

Why do we have spiritual gifts? What is our purpose in having them? The first thing that spiritual gifts do is to validate that we are messengers from the Lord in this world. Although Acts 1:8 points out that the Spirit's power is needed to be a witness of Jesus' resurrection from the dead, the five following Scriptures show that God's message was never meant to be "talk with no action" to those receiving it. Two of these passages deal with the more supernatural looking gifts —"signs, wonders, and miracles"— so it would be right to assume that these types of gifts are meant for this very purpose.

1. "For I would not dare say anything except what Christ has accomplished through me to make the Gentiles obedient by word and deed, by the power of miraculous signs and wonders, and by the power of God's Spirit.." — Romans 15:18-19, HCSB

2. "My speech and my proclamation were not with persuasive words of wisdom, but with a powerful demonstration by the Spirit, so that your faith might not be based on men's wisdom but on God's power." — 1 Corinthians 2:4-5, HCSB

3. "The signs of a true apostle were performed among you with all perseverance, by signs and wonders and miracles." — 2 Corinthians 12:12, NASB

4. "We know, dear brothers and sisters, that God loves you and has chosen you to be his own people. For when we brought you the

Good News, it was not only with words but also with power." — 1 Thessalonians 4:4-5, NLT

5. "For the kingdom of God is not in word, but in power." — 1 Corinthians 4:20, KJV

Since there were a lot of religions and philosophers in the various countries and cultures of the first century, the power of the Holy Spirit was needed to validate the apostles' message as being from the one true God.

The second purpose of any spiritual gift is to "build up the church." In 1 Corinthians 14:12 (HCSB), Paul says: "Since you are zealous for spiritual gifts, seek to excel in building up the church." Although the gifts that appear to be supernatural are needed for this purpose, too, this is often the more common role of the non-supernatural looking gifts, such as mine.

In Ephesians 2:19-22 (HCSB), there are two kinds of "building up the church" mentioned in the same passage. There is the increase of the numbers of the people coming into the church, and there is the spiritual development of the individual for the in-dwelling of the Spirit.

In the *Holman Christian Standard Bible*, this Scripture reads: "You are no longer foreigners and strangers, but fellow citizens with the saints, and members of God's household, built on the foundation of the apostles and prophets, with Christ Jesus Himself as the cornerstone. The whole building, being put together by Him, grows into a holy sanctuary in the Lord. You also are being built together for God's dwelling in the Spirit."

Just how God builds us up, and some gifts that he uses to do that, are outlined in Ephesians 4:11-13 (NLT): "Now these are the gifts Christ gave to the church: the apostles, the prophets, the evangelists, and the pastors and teachers. Their responsibility is to equip God's people to do his work and build up the church, the body of Christ. This will continue until we all come to such unity in our faith and knowledge of God's Son that we will be mature in the Lord, measuring up to the full and complete standard of Christ."

1 Corinthians 14:3-4 (NLT) compares the gift of speaking in tongues with the gift of prophecy, but helps us understand how each gift builds up the church in two different ways — strengthening ourselves and strengthening others. It says: "If you have the ability to speak in tongues, you will be talking only to God, since people won't be able to understand you. You will be speaking by the power of the Spirit, but it will all be mysterious. But one who prophesies strengthens others, encourages them, and comforts them. A person who speaks in tongues is strengthened personally, but one who speaks a word of prophecy strengthens the entire church."

Remember how Melanie's message to me from my dad broke down mental strongholds and years of bitterness that I had? This is an excellent example of how mediumship brought strengthening and comfort to me by getting rid of those things that blocked my spiritual growth. And that is this purpose of a spiritual gift being fulfilled.

The third purpose of a spiritual gift is to bring glory to Jesus. Jesus says of the Spirit in John 16:14-15 (HCSB): "He will glorify me, because he will take from what is mine and declare it to you. Everything the Father has is mine. This is why I told you that he takes from what is mine and will declare it to you."

In Acts 3, a lame man was healed at the gate to the temple. The crowd looked upon Peter and John in astonishment. Speaking in words given by the Spirit, Peter told them, "People of Israel," he said, in Acts 3:12 and 16 (NLT), "what is so surprising about this? And why stare at us as though we had made this man walk by our own power or godliness? . . . Through faith in the name of Jesus, this man was healed — and you know how crippled he was before. Faith in Jesus' name has healed him before your very eyes."

Since Jesus is the only way to salvation and becoming a part of God's people, glorifying Jesus leads to "building up the church" in numbers. I should be clear here: A church is not a building, a religion, a denomination of a religion, or necessarily the followers of one particular pastor or leader. It is a group of like-minded believers who share a common faith and bond with each other. They can be localized, but in these days of the Internet and social networks, they can be anywhere in the world.

Now that you understand the purposes of spiritual gifts, it is equally important for you to understand that the Bible requires that you put your gift to use and be accountable to the Lord for the use of your gift. Because of the many mediums and psychically gifted persons who have hidden their gifts in fear, I have written this book so that you *can openly use your gifts* to fulfill this requirement of the God who gave them to you.

The Bible says in Luke 12:48 (NASB): "From everyone who has been given much, much will be required; and to whom they entrusted much, of him they will ask all the more." 1 Timothy 4:14 (HCSB) says: "Do not neglect the gift that is in you."

In the parable of the talents (Matthew 25:14-30) the Lord brings out this point more clearly. In Jesus' time, "talent" didn't refer to an ability as it does today. A talent was a unit of money, a measurement of gold or silver used as currency. In this parable, a master calls three of his servants and entrusts them with differing amounts of money. To one he gives five talents, to another two talents, and to the last one he gives one talent. The man with the five talents puts them to work and earns five more. Likewise, the man with the two talents earns two more. But the man with the one talent hides his, for fear of losing it if his investment failed. The master praises the first two servants, but condemns the one who hid his talent.

The master told the servant who hid his talent that he should have at least put it on deposit with the bankers, so that when he returned he could have received interest on the talent. In the same way, just be willing to use your spiritual gift. Let the Holy Spirit do the work of helping you put it to use. As I said earlier, if it is a non-supernatural looking gift, you may have to be willing to assist others in serving Christ, so that others can see where you are gifted and let you know in what way you are gifted.

We are not given our spiritual gifts to hide them. If you have no idea about how to use your gift, it is time to pray and ask the Lord to make a way or show you a way. This was the case with my wife, who has a gift of predicting death. We at first had no idea how to use this gift without getting a morbid reputation. But we prayed about it and let God do it. Within a year two persons were given hope and comfort from this gift.

In the first case, Melanie was in the hospital in November of 2010, and she told me that she felt that her body was shutting down. I told her, "You're not going to die. You know how Stanna can predict death and she has said nothing of the kind about you." This gave her hope, which must have affected her body's healing processes, because soon thereafter her health began to turn around and she made a recovery.

Here is how this gift was a benefit a second time: One evening in the summer of 2011, I went to see an elderly couple who were in

Kevin Schoeppel

the class that I taught, to take them to the viewing for another class member who had passed away a few days before. The wife, whom I will call, Mary (not her real name), was the only member of my church who knew about Stanna's gift of predicting death. Stanna had told her personally about it a year and a half earlier.

On the way to the viewing we stopped for some food, and while we were eating Mary asked me this hypothetical question: "If you had information from the Lord that you were going to die on a specific date, and from a known cause, what if you were to subvert the Lord's plans by committing suicide at a different time? Would that invalidate the Lord's plans?"

I first replied by quoting what Job said to the Lord, in Job 42:2 (HCSB): "I know that you can do anything and no plan of yours can be thwarted." So something would happen to thwart the human attempt to change God's plan. I told her that the Lord may not even reveal such information to a person who is intent on defying God. I also shared with her the story of how King Saul had consulted a woman with a familiar spirit to contact the prophet Samuel, who told Saul that he would die in battle the next day. This came true even though Saul did not want it to happen.

Mary then confided to me that the real reason she asked that hypothetical question was because of an incident concerning her friend, whom we'll call, Nancy (not her real name). Stanna had predicted Nancy's death. A little more than a week before her death, Nancy had been quite talkative with Mary and had been good company to be around. But when Nancy's family went to see her a few days afterward, she was quiet and less responsive, and they wanted to put Nancy into a care home.

Mary, who normally doesn't intervene in such matters, tried at that time to persuade Nancy's family that by taking Nancy to the strange surroundings of a care home they would hasten her death. She even offered to let Nancy move into her own home, which was a more familiar setting. Nevertheless, the family stood by their decision, and took Nancy to the care home where she died on February 28th.

Ever since that time, Mary had been haunted by the feeling that if she been more insistent to Nancy's family about not putting her in the care home, Nancy might have lived longer or even still be alive. I told her that it was God's plan to take Nancy home on February 28th, 2010, and that her efforts could not have changed what God had planned.

"How on Earth did you remember the date of her death?" Mary asked me.

"Because it was on Sunday, January 31st, that Stanna told me, 'She'll be gone in a month,'" I told Mary. "Stanna does not normally know the exact date. In fact, this is rather rare, and now I can see why the Lord gave her that information. It was to set your mind at ease, by knowing it was His plan."

Mary replied, "I knew the Lord gave Stanna that gift and that she knew Nancy would pass away. But this is the first time you ever told me that she said this. I do feel now that it was God's plan to take her home. And that really is comforting to me."

You can now see how a spiritual gift of being able to predict death could be put to use in bringing hope and comfort to people. As I said before, at one time we had no idea how to put this gift to use. This was a perfect example of what the Lord meant when he said, as we are told in Isaiah 55:8-9 (NASB): "My thoughts are not your thoughts, nor are your ways my ways," declares the Lord. "For as the heavens are higher than the earth, so are my ways higher than your ways, and my thoughts are higher than your thoughts." No matter what spiritual gifts the Holy Spirit gives to you, and no matter how much you cannot possibly see how those gifts could be used to build people up, the Lord knows. And He is just waiting for you to ask Him.

Remember Tami, my girlfriend who had a gift for predicting the outcome of a football game? That couldn't be of the Lord, could it? How could predicting football games possibly build up God's people or bring them strengthening, encouragement and comfort?

In giving her the ability to predict the future, no matter how seemingly insignificant in the bigger picture of things, God — in His *infinite* knowledge of the future — knew that someday you would pick up this book and knew that it would somehow give you knowledge, encouragement, and comfort.

Those predictions by my psychic friend, Tami, were not *directly* for strengthening, encouragement, and comfort, but were allowed to come forth so that it would lead to me doing that for you as you read this. We can never know what route God has planned for a particular gift to reach its intended purpose. So we cannot say that a gift is not of God just because we cannot see it immediately doing one of these things.

EIGHT

Fulfilling Your Gifted Role

One afternoon Stanna had a dilemma. She had put some goslings out in a pen that was a former dog run, but the goslings were slipping out through the holes in the chain link fence. To prevent them from escaping, we would have to put up some chicken wire over the chain link fencing. I had just gotten home from work and was tired and really didn't want to do the job. But Stanna's friend's three daughters were there that day and were willing to help — Jolene, age eight; Pam, age ten; and Tiffany, age fifteen — and so I was willing to get started since I wouldn't have the burden of doing the whole job myself.

We needed sixty feet of chicken wire, but only had thirty-three feet of the three foot high chicken wire. Since we didn't need to have the chicken wire that high, the logical solution to this problem was to cut the chicken wire in half lengthwise. So that's what we did. It's harder than it sounds, because once you get past the first few feet of cutting, each cut half curls, gets heavy, and starts snagging on the rest of the wire. So the two younger girls, Pam and Jolene, started loosely rolling up the cut halves while Tiffany kept backing them up and having her younger sisters roll up the halves to keep pace with my cutting until we were done.

Then I put Tiffany in charge of tying the chicken wire to the fence with pieces of steel tie-wire, while I nailed the ends of the wire to the wooden posts with U-nails. Meanwhile, Pam was getting tie-wire pieces ready for Tiffany, while Jolene kept me supplied with U-nails. Their mother, Betsy, was there as well and brought me the tools I needed, and she took back the tools that I no longer needed as we went along. Once my nailing was done, I took over

Kevin Schoeppel

supplying Tiffany with the tie-wire needed to finish the job. By each person doing the parts of the job they could do best, we were done in eighty minutes.

In 1 Corinthians 12:12-16 (NLT), Paul used the parts of the body as an analogy to explain how different persons, with their different spiritual gifts, are needed and are supposed to work together: "The human body has many parts, but the many parts make up one whole body. So it is with the body of Christ. Some of us are Jews, some are Gentiles, some are slaves, and some are free. But we have all been baptized into one body by one Spirit, and we all share the same Spirit. Yes, the body has many different parts, not just one part. If the foot says, "I am not a part of the body because I am not a hand," that does not make it any less a part of the body. And if the ear says, "I am not part of the body because I am not an eye," would that make it any less a part of the body?"

When we think about spiritual gifts, quite often psychic ability, mediumship, or healing might come to mind first. Many Christians also think of the ability to speak in different tongues, wisdom, performing miracles, and discerning of spirits when thinking of spiritual gifts. But these are just the spiritual gifts that seem to get the most attention, mainly because they appear more supernatural and mysterious in nature. As we saw in the last chapter there are thirty-one gifts listed in the Bible, plus whatever Jesus did and promised his followers that they would be able to do. (See John 14:12).

Gifts of apostleship, teaching, pastoring, ability to help others, administration, encouraging, leadership, contributing to the needs of others, mercy, evangelism, and craftsmanship are all valid spiritual gifts. Even the ability to enjoy your work is a gift from God. Ecclesiastes 5:19 (NLT) says: "To enjoy your work and accept your lot in life — this is indeed a gift from God." It's just that some of these other gifts don't look to others as if it takes some special power from God to do them. But to those that have these gifts, they know differently, as we have already discussed.

Every follower of Jesus has at least one spiritual gift. And it is possible for any believer to have more than one spiritual gift, because 1 Corinthians 14:1 (NLT) says: "Desire the special abilities the Spirit gives — especially the ability to prophesy." Not only is "abilities" plural, but it remains a command even if you already have one spiritual gift.

However, even though the Scripture says "especially the ability to prophesy," we still do not have a choice in which gift or gifts we receive. The Bible says: "It is the one and only Spirit who distributes all these gifts. He alone decides which gift each person should have." (I Corinthians 12:11, NLT)

But there is not one particular spiritual gift that *all* followers of Jesus *would have* to have which would identify a person as one of his followers. This is what Paul was saying when he wrote: "If the foot says, "I am not a part of the body because I am not a hand," that does not make it any less a part of the body" Unfortunately, this is not what some churches teach, and this can cause doubts in some people as to whether they belong to the Lord or not.

The Assembly of God churches, for example, state in their Official Statement of Fundamental Truths: "We believe the Baptism in the Holy Spirit, [and] the initial physical evidence of the Baptism in the Holy Spirit is 'Speaking in Tongues.'"

But what if you just don't speak in tongues? Is something wrong if you do not have the gift of speaking in tongues? Does it mean God rejected you? No, you are not rejected. You just don't have that particular gift and that is all. In 1 Corinthians 12:29 (KJV),

Kevin Schoeppel

Paul asks: "Do all speak with tongues?" The implied answer here is "No."

Later on Paul says: "I wish that you all spoke in tongues, but even more that you would prophesy." (1 Corinthians 14:5, NASB) By saying "I *wish that you all spoke with tongues*," he *had* to mean, of course, that not all followers of Jesus would have this gift. He *wished* that they did, but they didn't.

But the bigger problem that Paul was dealing with was that some believers were acting as if their own particular spiritual gift meant that they were more important to God than someone with a different gift. For example, a person with the gift of enjoying their work might have felt like they were nothing compared to a medium or a healer. I know this feeling quite well. Many times I have sat around a table talking with friends and family members when that sneaky feeling of inferiority hits me: *You're the only one here who isn't psychic.* Just when I start thinking, "I wish I were psychic like them," then Stanna, or whomever, will just happen to say, "I can't recite the Bible the way you do, Kevin."

From God's perspective (God who is all-powerful, and surpasses all knowledge), the gift he gave you is what He feels is the right gift for you to do what he called you to do. To Him, it is unimportant whether the gift seems more amazing to others. How does it feel to *you*? And what do *you* do with it?

In the parable of the talents from the last chapter, the master wasn't saying that the man who received five talents was more important than the person who had two talents, or even more important than the person who got the one talent and hid it. He gave them what he wanted them to have and expected them to use what they had.

God knows exactly why He made you the way He made you, and why He gave you the gifts that He did. The Bible tells us that God says: "Do you question what I do for my children? Do you give me orders about the work of my hands?" (Isaiah 45:11, NLT)

Among the psychics and mediums I have known or have become acquainted with, nearly all of them have had a time in their lives when they wished they did not have the gifts that they have. The point to understand is that the Lord your God put those gifts into you for His own reasons that we are not to question. He didn't give me your gifts, but He may not have given you mine. My wife didn't want her gift of predicting death, but since God put that in her, and we knew she was accountable to Him for using her gift. We prayed about it, and you read of how God found at least two ways for that gift to bring glory to him that we never thought of.

Now let's go back to my story about the chicken wire. The girls were willing to help me, but they could not figure out what was needed, nor how to "make-do" with the materials at hand. On the other hand, I could picture what we needed to do, and how to end up with what we needed. But I was tired, it was hot, and to face having to do it all by myself seemed daunting.

This is why we really needed each other. What if we all had the enthusiasm to do the work, but nobody had any plan of what to do? Or what if we all had a plan for how to modify the dog run for goslings, but nobody wanted to jump in and get started?

This is the idea behind Paul's statement about gifts: "If the whole body were an eye, how would you hear? Or if your whole body were an ear, how would you smell anything? But our bodies have many parts, and God has put each part just where he wants it. How strange a body would be if it had only one part! Yes, there are many parts, but only one body." (1 Corinthians 12:17-20, NLT)

Although there may be readers of this book who are mediums or healers, the Lord knows that not everybody can be the medium or the healer. He has many other tasks that He wants carried out, and other types of gifts to give to the workers doing them so they can do His will. However, even though all persons are equally needed by God, not all *gifts* are of the same greatness, because the Bible says: "Prophecy is greater than speaking in tongues, unless someone interprets what you are saying, so that the whole church will be strengthened." (1 Corinthians 14:5 NLT)

What makes one gift greater than another gift? It is in *how much it builds up or benefits others* — *not* in how supernatural the gift seems to others. 1 Corinthians 14:12 (HCSB) says: "Since you are zealous for spiritual gifts, seek to excel in building up the church." The Spirit still determines what gifts we receive, but this verse seems to indicate that we can pray for what gifts we want. And if so, Paul is saying to desire gifts that build up the church.

But *all gifts are needed*, whether greater or lesser, as Paul goes on to say in 1 Corinthians 12:21-26 (NLT): "The eye can never say to the hand, 'I don't need you.' The head can't say to the feet, 'I don't need you.' In fact, some parts of the body that seem weakest and least important are actually the most necessary. And the parts we regard as less honorable are those we clothe with the greatest care. So we carefully protect those parts that should not be seen, while the more honorable parts do not require this special care. So God has put the body together such that extra honor and care are given to those parts that have less dignity. This makes for harmony among the members, so that all the members care for each other. If one part suffers, all the parts suffer with it, and if one part is honored, all the parts are glad."

Do you remember how Jolene and Pam, the two youngest girls, had to keep the chicken wire rolled up as I made each cut of the chicken wire, while their older sister watched over them doing it? To someone watching this, and to themselves, their job may not have seemed to be very important. But I badly needed the help of the younger girls to keep the individual halves of the chicken wire separated. Imagine cutting thirty-three feet of chicken wire one inch at a time without them —that's about 400 snips of the tin snips — while the parts already cut would be flopping in any direction, getting tangled and snagged on other parts of the wire fencing. Remember, it was a hot afternoon and I was tired, not in any mood for this kind of frustration. Yet, that is what I would have had without them.

And after the chicken wire was cut, I had the girls bring the rolled-up halves to the old dog run while I got different tools out. Even here, imagine me stretching out eighteen feet of chicken wire on one side all by myself. Maybe I could have done it by myself with some tool to hold one end of the wire in place, but it was a lot easier to ask Pam to hold the chicken wire at one end of the dog run while I stretched it out to the other end. Meanwhile, I assigned Jolene the task of handing me the U-nails I needed to anchor the wire to the wooden posts.

They felt good to be helping, and because they were, my stress was down and my job easier. All they had to do was to be willing to follow the orders that they were capable of doing according to their ability. For example, their older sister, Tiffany, was more adept at using the lineman's pliers to tie steel tie-wire to attach the stretched-out chicken wire to the chain-link fence. And so while Jolene continued to give me U-nails, Pam was given the new job of taking the tin-snips and cutting six inch pieces of steel tie-wire to keep her older sister well supplied and to keep the job flowing smoothly.

But what if any of them were told, "I don't need you!" or one of them wanted to do a different job than the one I gave them? It would have made it a harder, more frustrating job on a miserably hot afternoon. It wouldn't have been impossible but it definitely would have been harder. And perhaps the quality of the work

Kevin Schoeppel

would have suffered. But as it was, with everyone doing their part, we were done in less than an hour and a half, and the goslings were happily enjoying their new pen.

Paul had earlier told the Corinthian church: "After all, who is Apollos? Who is Paul? We are only God's servants through whom you believed the Good News. Each of us did the work the Lord gave us. I planted the seed in your hearts, and Apollos watered it, but it was God who made it grow. It's not important who does the planting, or who does the watering. What's important is that God makes the seed grow. The one who plants and the one who waters work together with the same purpose. And both will be rewarded for their own hard work. For we are both God's workers. And you are God's field. You are God's building. Because of God's grace to me, I have laid the foundation like an expert builder. Now others are building on it. But whoever is building on this foundation must be very careful." (1 Corinthians 3:5-10, NLT)

+ + + + +

When you stay at a hotel, no matter what hotel it is, what is the most important thing to you during your stay, and what is the thing that will make you want to stay again? That's right. . .a clean room, with a comfortable, pleasant bed, and a well-stocked bathroom. And whose job is it in the hotel to take care of that? Is it the manager's? Or maybe it's the assistant manager's? Of course not. It's housekeeping's job, which seems to be the lowest-level job in the hotel. They are the people treated as if they're the "bottom of the barrel," and are paid the lowest wages.

Yet all that the hotel spends on advertising would amount to nothing if it were not for the job of housekeeping to bring repeat business and spread positive "word-of-mouth" advertising.

Not long after a tragic elementary school shooting was in the news, I was talking with my son, Ryan, about how his "quick visions" of a soon-to-happen scene in the future could be a real lifesaving benefit. "Suppose, son, that you have one of your 'quick visions' and it happens to be a shooting. You wouldn't necessarily have to be armed and at the scene of the shooting to 'take out' the killer in order to save lives. If you happen to recognize who the person is, you could perhaps meet them days or hours before the shooting, talk to them, and maybe diffuse the anger in them so that the shooting never happens. Or you could persuade them to spend time with you having fun doing something else at the time the shooting was to take place, so it never happens. Because no shooting would happen to make the news, nobody would call you a hero — but the God who gave you your ability would know you were a hero and reward you."

In short, no one person's task — or the spiritual gift given to that person to accomplish their task — is more important than the other person's. Note that Paul said: "The one who plants and the one who waters work together with the same purpose. And both will be rewarded for their own hard work." If you do your work, you will be rewarded. You do not need to do the other person's work in order to receive your reward.

God is not unjust. He will not forget how hard you have worked for him and how you have shown your love to him by caring for other believers, as you still do. — Hebrews 6:10, (NLT)

Kevin Schoeppel

NINE
Working For The Lord: Benefits & Pay

Did you know you were created for work? Ephesians 2:10 (NASB) says: "For we are His workmanship, created in Christ Jesus for good works, which God prepared beforehand so that we would walk in them." Psalm 139:14 and 16 (HCSB) say: "I will praise you because I have been remarkably and wonderfully made. Your works are wonderful, and I know this very well. All my days were written in your book and planned before a single one of them began."

When you put these Scriptures together, God is saying that you are a special person, "remarkably and wonderfully made" for a special task that he determined you were the right person for, long before you were ever born. Many of us though, wonder if we really are doing the work God intended for us to be doing. Are we supposed to be actively seeking whatever it is ourselves? If we encounter obstacles, is it the Lord's way of saying we're on the wrong track? Or are these obstacles and difficulty part of preparing us for that work? And whether the pay is enough to make a living or not — is that any sign from God we are doing the work he wants us to do?

Jesus said, "You did not choose me but I chose you, and appointed you that you would go and bear fruit." (John 15:16, NASB) Notice that Jesus did not say "produce fruit." That is the Spirit's job. But we are the human instruments that the Spirit of the Lord uses to accomplish his work. Scripture says: "There are different kinds of spiritual gifts, but the same Spirit is the source of them all. There are different kinds of service, but we serve the same Lord." (1 Corinthians 12:4-5, NLT). And Scripture also says: "God is working in you, giving you the desire and the power to do what pleases him." (Philippians 2:13, NLT)

Many people struggle with finding their life's purpose, the right career, or with finding a job that is more fulfilling than one already has. But with the aforesaid in mind we don't really need to concern ourselves with trying to find out what our work is. The Spirit knows that. And Scripture does emphasize that we allow the Spirit to lead us. Romans 8:14 (KJV) says: "For as many as are led by the Spirit of God, they are the sons of God," and "If we live in the Spirit, let us also walk in the Spirit." (Galatians 5:25, KJV) So if we simply follow the Spirit, *he* will see to it that we are doing the right work. However, this doesn't mean that the right work will come to us immediately.

In 1989, I visited a local Assembly of God church, A person there with the gift of prophesy had a message for me: "God has something special for you to do, Kevin, but you must first learn to obey." I had to make up my mind to obey God. And I can honestly say that the Holy Spirit has opened up the opportunities for me to serve God one at a time, as he determined I was ready for doing them. These were but steps on the path to reaching and teaching the "right work."

Difficulties and hardships in the work are part of our training for the work, not an indication we are on the "wrong" track. In the *Old Testament* it says: "Though the Lord give you the bread of adversity, and the water of affliction. . .thine eyes shall see thy teachers: and thine ears shall hear a word behind thee, saying, This is the way, walk ye in it, when ye turn to the right hand, and when ye turn to the left.'" (Isaiah 30:20-21, KJV)

Jesus said about the Apostle Paul: "I will show him how much he must suffer for my name's sake." (Acts 9:16, NASB) And he did suffer, for later on Paul himself said: "Five different times the

Jewish leaders gave me thirty-nine lashes. Three times I was beaten with rods. Once I was stoned. Three times I was shipwrecked. Once I spent a whole night and a day adrift at sea. I have traveled on many long journeys. I have faced danger from rivers and from robbers. I have faced danger from my own people, the Jews, as well as from the Gentiles. I have faced danger in the cities, in the deserts, and on the seas. And I have faced danger from men who claim to be believers but are not. I have worked hard and long, enduring many sleepless nights. I have been hungry and thirsty and have often gone without food. I have shivered in the cold, without enough clothing to keep me warm. Then, besides all this, I have the daily burden of my concern for all the churches." (2 Corinthians 11:24-28, NLT).

Why do college students endure the load of work for the courses they are taking? It is so they will be prepared to do the work they want to do in their life, and they know this is part of "paying their dues." It's no different when we work for the Lord, even though we may not understand what he is preparing us for. Just a few years ago I never imagined that I would be writing this book that you are now reading. But without knowing that, I resolved to obey God, and be led by the Spirit. And here we are. The Holy Spirit has brought every idea to mind, and reminded me of the Scriptures needed for supporting that which you read here now.

Proverbs 3:5-6 (KJV) applies here: "Trust in the Lord with all thine heart; and lean not unto thine own understanding. In all thy ways acknowledge him, and he shall direct thy paths." Whenever I gave the Lord the credit, he continued to guide the teaching work I was doing. Sometimes, even while driving to the church, I just asked for the Holy Spirit's help because I had tried to prepare a lesson and had trouble doing it. Every time, the Holy Spirit took over, and the class went well. And so in the end, I would admit that the Holy Spirit had done the actual teaching.

Have you ever asked yourself: *If I am really doing the work I'm supposed to be doing for the Lord, wouldn't the Lord make a way for me to be getting paid enough from it to be able to do that work full-time? Aren't I supposed to have complete and total support, and everything I need to do the Lord's work or to do whatever He wants me to do?*

To a man who wanted to follow him wherever he went, Jesus once said: "Foxes have holes, and birds of the air have nests; but the Son of man hath not where to lay his head." (Luke 9:58, KJV) In all of his preaching and ministering to others, he never had a place to live himself. Jesus did his ministry full time, but instead of payment he received the support of others to meet both his needs and that of his disciples.

In Luke 9:3-4 (NLT), Jesus sent out his twelve disciples and told them: "Take nothing for your journey. Don't take a walking stick, a traveler's bag, food, money, or even a change of clothes. Wherever you go, stay in the same house until you leave town." Why? In a parallel passage, Matthew 10:8 (NASB), Jesus adds: ". . .for the worker is worth his support." Jesus considered being offered room and board as something that the disciples rightfully earned for the work they were doing for Him. Jesus himself was invited to stay with Peter and Andrew (Mark 1:29), Simon the Leper (Mark 14:3), Simon the Pharisee (Luke 7:36), Zacchaeus (Luke 19:9), Mary, Martha and Lazarus (John 12:1), and "one of the rulers of the Pharisees." (Luke 14:21)

What if no one was willing to take in Jesus or his disciples? This did happen once. In Luke 9:52-56, the people in a village in Samaria refused him a place to stay because he was a Jew on his way to Jerusalem. But Jesus simply went to another village.

Jesus also had financial help, too. In Luke 8:1-3 (NLT), we read: "Jesus began a tour of the nearby towns and villages, preaching and announcing the Good News about the Kingdom of God. He took his twelve disciples with him, along with some women who had been cured of evil spirits and diseases. Among them were Mary Magdalene, from whom he had cast out seven demons; Joanna, the wife of Chuza, [King] Herod's business manager; Susanna; and many others who were contributing from their own resources to support Jesus and his disciples." Gratitude for being healed and having demons exorcised from them was probably a good reason they supported him. While Jesus did not charge money for such things, he also did not refuse generosity from those who wished to do something for him.

Since her husband was the business manager for King Herod, Joanna was probably quite wealthy. And she is rewarded for her financial support, because in Luke 24:10, Joanna and Mary Magdalene are two of the very first people to see the two angels at Jesus' tomb, and receive the news that Jesus had risen from the dead.

The Apostle Paul did things differently. He was in a different part of the world (Greece), in which he was a foreigner in a land with different customs than that of the Jews with whom he had grown up with in Tarsus, or while he was a student in Jerusalem. Paul was aware, like Jesus, that he had earned the *right* to expect at least room and board for the work he was doing. He had written to the church at Corinth: "If we have sown spiritual things for you, is it too much if we reap material benefits from you? If others have this right to receive benefits from you, don't we even more?" (1 Corinthians 9:11-12, HCSB). But he continues: "However, we have not made use of this right; instead we endure everything so that we will not hinder the gospel of Christ."

Why did Paul make the choice to not accept any pay — not *even* room and board — for preaching the Gospel? His first reason was to separate himself from others who were "in it for the money." Paul wrote to them later in 2 Corinthians 2:17 (NLT): "You see, we are not like the many hucksters who preach for personal profit. We preach the word of God with sincerity and with Christ's authority, knowing that God is watching us." There were a lot of pagan religions in Greece (see Acts 17:16), and apparently the leaders in those pagan practices were charging for what they were doing. It seemed to Paul that if he were to preach the Gospel of Christ for no charge, the people could see he had no ulterior motives of taking their money.

His second reason to not accept pay or support was that he wanted to show that his love for them was genuine. "Now I am coming to you for the third time and I will not be a burden to you," Paul writes, in 2 Corinthians 12:14-15 (NLT): "I don't want what you have — I want you. After all, children don't provide for their parents. Rather, parents provide for their children. I will gladly spend myself and all I have for you, even though it seems that the more I love you, the less you love me." He used this analogy of a parent who loves his or her children to show the kind of love he had for the Corinthians.

He felt the same toward the people at Thessalonica: "As apostles of Christ we certainly had a right to make some demands of you, but instead we were like children among you. Or we were like a mother feeding and caring for her own children. We loved you so much that we shared with you not only God's Good News but our own lives, too." (1 Thessalonians 2:7-8, NLT). Genuine love from a person can make quite a difference in the way we see them. It's quite true the old adage that "people don't care how much you know, until they know how much you care."

His third reason to not accept pay or support was to set an example. At the church in Thessalonica, there were lazy people who were going around "mooching" off of others. Paul wrote and reminded them: "You know that you ought to imitate us. We were not idle when we were with you. We never accepted food from anyone without paying for it. We worked hard day and night so we would not be a burden to any of you. We certainly had the right to ask you to feed us, but we wanted to give you an example to follow.

"Even while we were with you, we gave you this command: 'Those unwilling to work will not get to eat.' Yet we hear that some of you are living idle lives, refusing to work and meddling in other people's business. We command such people and urge them in the name of the Lord Jesus Christ to settle down and work to earn their own living." (2 Thessalonians 3:7-12, NLT)

If Paul would not accept pay or support in his work for the Lord, how did Paul provide a living for himself? In Acts 18:1-3, we find out that his trade was tent making. When Paul said that he "worked very hard night and day," he was first doing his work by day as a tentmaker to earn money, and then doing the work by night that the Lord had called him to do.

Today it is unfortunate that our society only considers us to *be* whatever we get *paid* for doing — and anything else we do is deemed "volunteer work" or "community service." History has proven, though, that this social view did not hold true for Paul. He never received — nor would he accept — one penny for being an apostle of Jesus Christ. Fourteen times in the *New Testament* he is called an apostle, two of those times is called "an apostle and a herald," and once "an apostle, a herald, and a teacher. " (2 Timothy 1:11)

Only Acts 18:3 mentions the tent making — and only as a passing explanation of why he stayed with Priscilla and Aquila, since they both did that kind of work too. Few people today even give a thought to how many tents he made, what types he sold, what customers he had, or how expensive they were. But his "volunteer work"— being an apostle — *was his actual occupation.* And that is what Paul is forever remembered for.

Have you ever taken a walk through a cemetery and read what is on the headstones? What do you find out about the life of the person whose body is buried there? One day when I arrived early at Eastlawn Cemetery in Tucson to do a funeral service, I walked around and did just that. Most men had something on their headstones that denoted that they served their country, or that they were a "beloved father" or "beloved grandfather." Women were remembered as a "beloved mother" or "beloved grandmother." On the way back to the chapel I happened to look in the mausoleum, and I recognized the name of a man who had owned one of the most successful appliance dealerships in Tucson back in the 1960s. *For all of his success as a businessman, there was nothing on his tomb to indicate what he had done for a living.* If not for my own memory, I would not have known.

We are not defined by our job title. We are what we have become to the people who know and love us. And that is with pay or no pay, and with money or not.

So far I have limited the discussion of pay to what we receive here and now in this life. Hebrews 6:10 (NLT) says: "God is not unjust. He will not forget how hard you have worked for him and how you have shown your love to him by caring for other believers, as you still do." Jesus said: "Do not work for the food which perishes, but for the food which endures to eternal life, which the Son of Man will give to you, for on Him the Father, God, has set His seal." (John 6:27, NASB) And in Matthew 16:27 (KJV), Jesus says: "For the Son of man shall come in the glory of his Father with his angels; and then he shall reward every man according to his works." So we may not necessarily get compensated for our spiritual work during *this* life.

Paul, who never accepted pay for being a disciple, said: "If our hope in Christ is only for this life, we are more to be pitied than anyone in the world." (1 Corinthians 15:19, NLT) But he wrote to Timothy just before he was beheaded in Rome: "Now the prize awaits me — the crown of righteousness, which the Lord, the righteous Judge, will give me on the day of his return. And the prize is not just for me but for all who eagerly look forward to his appearing." (2 Timothy 4:8, NLT)

At our jobs many of us recognize the value of *deferred compensation* — of having our employer deduct part of our pay for retirement. Imagine having compensation deferred until we are with the Lord — beyond the other side, beyond the judgment — in Heaven. There are also material possessions to be had in Heaven. Jesus said: "Use your worldly resources to benefit others and make friends. Then, when your earthly possessions are gone, they will welcome you to an eternal home. And if you are untrustworthy about worldly wealth, who will trust you with the true riches of heaven? And if you are not faithful with other people's things, why should you be trusted with things of your own?" (Luke 16:9,11-12, NLT)

"True riches," and "things of your own," must be referring to what we receive in Heaven, because it is contrasted with "worldly wealth" and "other people's things." Although it is practically a cliché, Paul wrote in 1 Timothy 6:7 (KJV): "We brought nothing into this world, and it is certain we can carry nothing out."

Paul sums it up so well in 1 Timothy 6:17-19 (NLT), that I will make it our closing thoughts on work for the Lord: "Teach those who are rich in this world not to be proud and not to trust in their money, which is so unreliable. Their trust should be in God, who richly gives us all we need for our enjoyment. Tell them to use their money to do good. They should be rich in good works and generous to those in need, always being ready to share with others. By doing this they will be storing up their treasure as a good foundation for the future so that they may experience true life."

Kevin Schoeppel

TEN

What About My Gift?

If you are psychic, or if you are a medium, you may have wondered to yourself while reading the last chapter if I would answer the question: "Should I charge for a reading?" Is there a way to answer this from Scripture? Is it ethical or right to charge money for using any spiritual gift, not just psychic or mediumship ability? I have the spiritual gift of teaching, and you bought my book. So by accepting money for my book, am I doing what God considers to be right? Or am I disobeying God?

When Jesus sent out his twelve disciples, in Matthew 10:7-10 (NASB), he told them: "And as you go, preach, saying, 'The kingdom of heaven is at hand.' Heal the sick, raise the dead, cleanse the lepers, cast out demons. Freely you received, freely give. Do not acquire gold, or silver, or copper for your money belts, or a bag for your journey, or even two coats, or sandals, or a staff; for the worker is worthy of his support."

When Jesus said, "Freely you received, freely give," what was the "freely received" thing that he commanded them to "freely give?" Was he asking them to freely give money? No, because he told them, "Do not acquire any gold or silver or copper in your belts." They could not give something they didn't have. Note that "acquire," as it used here, referred to getting the gold or silver *before* they were sent out, not *during* their mission (See Luke 9:3).

He commands his disciples to preach that the kingdom of Heaven is near, and then to do certain supernatural tasks — heal the sick raise the dead, cleanse lepers and drive out demons — before he says to "freely give."

The preaching of the Gospel — that is, to preach that Jesus is the Christ, the Son of God, and that you will be able to enter the kingdom of Heaven only by accepting him as Lord and Savior — is always validated by the use of spiritual gifts. One job is never meant to be done without the other. So to "freely give" of supernatural power, as it is used in these verses, meant for them to do the job Jesus gave them to do. They were workers who were "worth their keep," so it would only be natural for them to receive something in return for their work, just as we do for our work. And those who were healed, perhaps felt obliged to provide the disciples some food and a place to stay, knowing that a doctor *would* have charged for the healing they received.

Our Lord set the example by doing this himself, because we read: "Jesus traveled through all the towns and villages of that area, teaching in the synagogues and announcing the Good News about the Kingdom. And he healed every kind of disease and illness. When he saw the crowds, he had compassion on them because they were confused and helpless, like sheep without a shepherd." (Matthew 9:35-36, NLT) And, as we read before, Jesus likewise freely gave, but did not refuse generosity in return.

But how can we "freely give" and still say, "the worker is worth his keep?" Are these things conflicting with each other? And am I "beating around the bush" on the issue of charging? No, because there really is not one particular Scripture that says, "You may charge money to use a spiritual gift," or that says, "It is wrong to charge money to use a spiritual gift." What really determines whether it is right or wrong to charge a price for using a spiritual gift is the thoughts and intents of your heart behind your decision to do so or not. Our culture of today is quite different from that of first-century Palestine. Hospitality is not the social norm, as it was then, and both the giver and receiver of healing, or any other spiritual benefit, today think in terms of money to pay for needs.

Kevin Schoeppel

So if you do charge for a reading, how much is right to charge? If you are not charging money, what should you expect in return for benefitting someone from your gift? The apostle Paul wrote on the idea of being paid for spiritual work. As you read previously, he not only would not accept pay for his work for the Lord, but went a step further by providing all of his own needs and not being a burden to anyone. *But this was his choosing.* In 1 Corinthians 9:4-7 (NASB), he wrote; "Do we not have a right to eat and drink? Do we not have a right to take along a believing wife, even as the rest of the apostles and the brothers of the Lord and Cephas? Or do only Barnabas and I not have a right to refrain from working? Who at any time serves as a soldier at his own expense? Who plants a vineyard and does not eat the fruit of it? Or who tends a flock and does not use the milk of the flock?"

He goes on to say: "The plowman ought to plow in hope, and the thresher to thresh in hope of sharing the crops. If we sowed spiritual things in you, is it too much if we reap material things from you?" (1 Corinthians 9:10-11, NASB)

If you work, you are entitled to benefit from your work. That is clear. One difference that Paul mentions is that of doing spiritual work and reaping a material harvest from that. Jesus was way ahead of Paul on this when he said: "Therefore take no thought, saying, what shall we eat? or, what shall we drink? or, wherewithal shall we be clothed?. . . for your Heavenly Father knoweth that ye have need of all these things. But seek ye first the kingdom of God, and his righteousness; and all these things shall be added unto you." (Matthew 6:31-33, KJV)

Clearly spiritual work comes first. Then material compensation follows. And God intends for us to expect — and receive — reasonable compensation for reasonable work. He would not be a just God if he did not. Our gifts are our equipment for doing his work. Just as my employer furnishes me a desk and computer for doing my work for him, the same is true of God and our spiritual gifts.

Greed, however, is wrong. Ephesians 5:5 says that no greedy person has any inheritance in the kingdom of God. And Colossians 3:5 (NASB) tells us to "Consider the members of your earthly body as dead to immorality, impurity, passion, evil desire, and greed, *which amounts to idolatry*."

Jesus talks about what greed is. Once, when he was speaking to his disciples near the temple in Jerusalem, a large crowd gathered around him and many religious leaders were present as well. Someone called from the crowd, "Teacher, please tell my brother to divide our father's estate with me."

Jesus replied, "Friend, who made me a judge over you to decide such things as that?" Then he said, "Beware! Guard against every kind of greed. Life is not measured by how much you own."

Then he told them a story as he so often did: "A rich man had a fertile farm that produced fine crops. He said to himself: 'What should I do? I don't have room for all my crops.' Then he said, 'I know! I'll tear down my barns and build bigger ones. Then I'll have room enough to store all my wheat and other goods. And I'll sit back and say to myself, 'My friend, you have enough stored away for years to come. Now take it easy! Eat, drink, and be merry!' But God said to him, 'You fool! You will die this very night. Then who will get everything you worked for?'" (Luke 12:13-20, NLT)

What caused Jesus to teach this about greed was a man fighting with his brother over an inheritance. Before the man's parents passed away, did he need their money to meet his needs? Probably not. Most adults are usually financially independent of their parents. If he were disinherited, would he become a beggar? Again, it is not likely.

This man may have seen his question as a request for Jesus to bring "fairness" between what his brother got and what he "should have." Pick any group of heirs fighting over an estate and not one of those persons will see themselves as greedy. No, they will tell you that they are trying to be fair. This is why Jesus says, "Guard against *every kind* of greed."

In the parable Jesus told about the rich man and the fertile farm, it sounds like the rich man was considering retirement. The parable does not tell us whether the rich man did the planting and harvesting himself, or if he hired men to do it. What it does tell us is that he had far more than he needed to meet his needs for many years. He had more than what he could store in his present barns. It would be normal for us to think: *How can this be greed? The man is concerned with a way to save that which he had rightfully earned.*

Two questions arise from this: If the rich man could not store it all himself, why didn't he consider giving the excess, which he could not store, to others who could have benefitted from it? And why would he need to tear down his old barns? Being obsessed with *needing* to have more than what it takes to provide for ourselves and our family in the present seems to be the problem.

In Matthew 6:11 (KJV), in the verses commonly known as "The Lord's Prayer," we read: "Give us this day our daily bread." The thought behind those words of Jesus goes back to the story about the manna that God provided for Israel in the Sinai wilderness. In that story Moses told the people of Israel: "It is the food the Lord has given you to eat. These are the Lord's instructions: 'Each household should gather as much as it needs. Pick up two quarts [of dry manna] for each person in your tent.'" So the people of Israel did as they were told. Some gathered a lot, some only a little. But when they measured it out, everyone had just enough. Those who gathered a lot had nothing left over, and those who gathered only a little had enough. Each family had just what it needed.

Then Moses told them, "Do not keep any of it until morning." But some of them didn't listen and kept some of it [manna] until morning. But by then it was full of maggots and had a terrible smell. Moses was very angry with them. After this the people gathered the food morning by morning, each family according to its need. And as the sun became hot, the flakes of manna which they had not picked up melted and disappeared.

On the sixth day, they gathered twice as much as usual — four [dry] quarts of manna for each person instead of two. Then all the leaders of the community came and asked Moses for an explanation. He told them, "This is what the Lord commanded: Tomorrow will be a day of complete rest, a holy Sabbath day set apart for the Lord. So bake or boil as much as you want today, and set aside what is left for tomorrow." So they put some aside until morning, just as Moses had commanded. And in the morning the leftover food was wholesome and good, without maggots or odor. Moses said, "Eat this food today, for today is a Sabbath day dedicated to the Lord. There will be no food on the ground today." (Exodus 16:15-25, NLT)

God intended to provide for each day's need as it came, with the exception of the Sabbath day. This is part of that relationship of trust that God wants to have with each of us. There is no certainty that we will have a tomorrow. Proverbs 27:1 (NASB) says: "Do not boast about tomorrow, for you do not know what a day may

Kevin Schoeppel

bring forth." In the Book of James, James says "Look here, you who say, "Today or tomorrow we are going to a certain town and will stay there a year. We will do business there and make a profit." How do you know what your life will be like tomorrow? Your life is like the morning fog — it's here a little while, then it's gone. What you ought to say is, 'If the Lord wants us to, we will live and do this or that.'" (James 4:13-15, NLT)

This was what the rich man on the fertile farm was overlooking. God called him a fool because his life was being taken from him that night. His life was over. And the time would be ahead when he would have to account for the gifts he was given in his life. "What did you do with that abundant crop I gave you?" God may very well ask. And what will the man's answer be?

Remember: "From everyone who has been given much, much will be required; and to whom they entrusted much, of him they will ask all the more." (Luke 12:48, NASB). At the judgment, the question will not be: "Did you charge money when you used your gifts?" but rather, "What did you do with the gifts I gave you?" The question doesn't only refer to spiritual gifts, but to material ones as well. And as we have learned, it is not wrong to reap material items from the use of spiritual gifts. We will be accountable for all of it.

Now, let's go back to Paul's discussion on benefitting from the work that we do. "Do you not know that those who perform sacred services eat the food of the temple, and those who attend regularly to the altar have their share from the altar? So also the Lord directed those who proclaim the gospel to get their living from the gospel." (1 Corinthians 9:13-14, NASB)

But he goes on to say: "But I have used none of these things. . .if I preach the gospel, I have nothing to boast of, for I am under compulsion; for woe is me if I do not preach the gospel. For if I do this voluntarily, I have a reward; but if against my will, I have a stewardship entrusted to me. What then is my reward? That, when I preach the gospel, I may offer the gospel without charge, so as not to make full use of my right in the gospel." (1 Corinthians 9:15-18, NASB)

Paul had a right to receive money or material goods for his work. His work, as an apostle, was to preach the gospel, with signs and wonders and miracles to accompany his preaching. When he says, "Woe is me if I do not preach the gospel!" he is restating what Jesus taught: that we must put our spiritual gifts to use. But in each case of using his gifts to serve God, he has a choice. He may use his rights in the present, or receive a reward from the Lord in the future. The rewards are how we become "rich toward God" in terms of working with our gifts.

An electronic search on the use of the word "reward" in the *New Testament* mostly associates the word with compensation from God and in the Kingdom of Heaven. The most obvious of these is Matthew 16:27 (KJV): "For the Son of man shall come in the glory of his Father with his angels; and then he shall reward every man according to his works."

Other scriptures of this kind are Matthew 6:2-6, Matthew 6:16-18, Mark 9:41, Luke 6:23, Luke 6:35, 1 Corinthians 3:14, Ephesians 6:8, Colossians 3:24, Hebrews 11:26, 2 John 1:8, Revelation 11:18 and Revelation 22:12. I encourage you to read these verses. As you meditate upon them, ask the Spirit to teach you more about the rewards of the work you do for the Lord.

In Luke 12:33 (NLT), Jesus uses the phrase "treasure in heaven" to illustrate converting our material goods into being rich toward God. "Sell your possessions and give to those in need. This will store up treasure for you in heaven! And the purses of heaven never get old or develop holes. Your treasure will be safe; no thief can steal it and no moth can destroy it." Mark 10:21 (NASB) says: "Go and sell all you possess and give to the poor, and you will have treasure in heaven; and come, follow Me." This is why the rich man was not "rich toward God." His only concern was how to keep all of the crops for himself. My class members were very quick to pick up the fact that he could at least have distributed what he couldn't store.

And so to sum up what Scripture has to say about charging money for use of your spiritual gifts: First, there is nothing wrong with earning the money to provide your living. You have the option, however, in every instance of using your gifts, to exercise your right to receive material support or to receive a reward from the Lord at a later time.

But it will always be wrong to disobey the Lord. We have not been taught enough in our present-day society about greed. In fact, modern society considers it good to be ambitious and to be as financially successful as we can be. And for that reason greed is a difficult thing for our consciences to recognize.

This is where we need to pray for the guidance of the Spirit, for as it says in John 16:7-10, it is his job to convict us of sin, righteousness, and judgment. He will convict us of greed when the world would tell us that we are doing the right thing. One way he does this is by whether or not we have peace within ourselves about what we are doing. Colossians 3:15 (KJV) says: "Let the peace of God rule in your hearts." This means that if we consider doing something that will cause us to disobey God, we will not have a feeling of peace proceeding doing it. Philippians 4:7 (NASB) says "The peace of God, which surpasses all comprehension, will guard your hearts and your minds in Christ Jesus."

Another scriptural self-determination method available to you is what is referred to as the "golden rule." Although almost all religions have some variation of it, Jesus was the only one to say it in the positive, proactive form as we know it today: "Do to others whatever you would like them to do to you. This is the essence of all that is taught in the law and the prophets." (Matthew 7:12, NLT)

Put yourself in the place of the person who has a need for you to use your gift. How do they feel about you charging for use of your gift? Is the price not only reasonable for the work you are doing, but affordable to them in their circumstances?

In a dire situation, such as in the case of a missing child, would you say it would be right then to expect to be paid before giving any information to the parents or the police, when others who aren't necessarily psychic and who are not expecting anything in return, are giving freely of their own time, resources, energies, to help get this child reunited with his or her parents? Of course, this is a much more dramatic situation than most you might encounter every day. Still, just putting yourself in the place of others is a great way to determine what is right to do in God's eyes.

Another dilemma for any psychic or medium would be whether to do readings or not. We read how it is clear from Scripture that we are not to consult persons with familiar spirits, but rather to seek the Lord's guidance. So what do you do if you are a medium or psychic, and someone comes to you for a reading?

Melanie does get asked for readings, and so I asked her how she handles them since she both serves the Lord and still does readings for people. First, she says she tries not to ask what religion they are. Then she explains what to expect to happen in a reading. They may not get their answers right away, or the spirit they expected to come through may not, or whichever spirit does come through may want to reach somebody else nearby instead. Because the person having their reading with Melanie is not dealing with a person "having a familiar spirit," the spirits are "calling the shots," and not Melanie herself, so results are unpredictable. She will also explain that she does not do relationship issues such as, "When will I meet the right man?" or questions that are greed-based such as, "Where is a certain valuable object hidden?"

But more importantly, she will explain that a reading from her should be a last resort. She will ask the person beforehand, "Did you pray to the Lord about this before you came to me? If not, why aren't you praying for your answer? Did you contact your pastor or minister before coming to me? Have you sought your own answers to what you are coming to me for?" She will also ask the thought-provoking question, "Why do you want to know the answer to the question you are asking?"

Melanie told me that although it would be great to make money doing readings all day, she has a sense of responsibility to the Lord as far as being the source of information to the person requesting the reading. By the time the person has answered her initial questions, if all other sources for answers have been exhausted, then she will tell them, "If this were not of God, then you would not be here."

And by this point, she would be right. Biblically, in 1 Samuel 9, Saul and his servant had been sent to look for his father's donkeys and had searched for three days with no results. It was the servant who encouraged Saul to go to Samuel the prophet, who was also called the "seer," to inquire as to which direction to go looking for the donkeys. Upon reaching the seer Samuel tells Saul, without asking why he came to him, "In the morning I will let you go, and will tell you all that is on your mind. As for your donkeys which were lost three days ago, do not set your mind on them, for they have been found." (1 Samuel 9:19-20, NASB) Unlike at the end of Saul's life, when he disobeyed God for consulting the woman with a familiar spirit at Endor, he obviously now was not disobeying God, because this encounter ultimately led to God's purpose of making him king over Israel.

Isaiah 8:19-20 (NASB) is not a command forbidding a reading, but rather puts forth a serious question to the person who is wanting the reading: "When they say to you, 'Consult the mediums and the spiritists who whisper and mutter,' should not a people consult their God? Should they consult the dead on behalf of the living? To the law and to the testimony! If they do not speak according to this word, it is because they have no dawn."

Melanie's question, "Did you pray to the Lord about this before you came to me?" is exactly what the Bible is saying in that verse, in a different way. *Why aren't you seeking the Lord in the first place?* This is her first step in spiritually re-orienting the person requesting the reading. Essentially, she turns a reading into a spiritual check-up for the one asking her for the reading, because she is aware that the Lord is holding her responsible as the source that the person has turned to. She must speak according to God's word.

Gaining recognition works on the same principle as charging money. You either are rewarded in the present, or rewarded in the future. Jesus has this to say about drawing attention to yourself: "When you give to someone in need, don't do as the hypocrites do — blowing trumpets in the synagogues and streets to call attention to their acts of charity! *I tell you the truth. They have received all the reward they will ever get.* But when you give to someone in need, don't let your left hand know what your right hand is doing. Give your gifts in private, and your Father, who sees everything, will reward you. When you pray, don't be like the hypocrites who love to pray publicly on street corners and in the synagogues where everyone can see them. *I tell you the truth, that is all the reward they will ever get*. But when you pray, go away by yourself, shut the door behind you, and pray to your Father in private. Then your Father, who sees everything, will reward you." (Matthew 6:2-6, NLT)

When the use of your gift awes people around you, or you develop a reputation for being right about things that you "couldn't have possibly known," word will spread like wildfire. The important thing to remember then is that if it were not for the Spirit of the Lord, you wouldn't have this gift that you do. And so you must give credit where credit is due.

Jesus had crowds following him everywhere, expecting healing and miracles. But he told them: "I tell you the truth, the Son can do nothing by himself. He does only what he sees the Father doing. Whatever the Father does, the Son also does." (John 5:19, NLT)

When Peter and John healed a lame man by the temple gate, Peter's answer to those in awe was: "People of Israel, what is so surprising about this? And why stare at us as though we had made this man walk by our own power or godliness? . . . Through faith in the name of Jesus, this man was healed — and you know how crippled he was before. Faith in Jesus' name has healed him before your very eyes." (Acts 3:12 and 16, NLT)

When anyone complimented me on a great Sunday school lesson, or a great sermon, I simply would tell them, "It was the Lord." I often don't know what to say other than, "*He* is the one who taught a great lesson."

+ + + + +

One Sunday we had a healing in our class. A woman, Thelma, had scheduled an appointment with her ophthalmologist for a severe pain behind her left retina. Although we had our opening prayer, about ten minutes into the lesson I stopped and felt we all needed to pray for healing for Thelma. We all laid hands on her and I led the prayer, which went something like this: "Lord, we pray that you would heal the pain behind Thelma's retina. We know you are a God of miracles, and that you have the ability to heal her. So, Lord, if it be your will, please heal her."

We then went back to the lesson. About ten minutes later I heard Thelma shout, "It's gone! That pain behind my retina that's been there since Thursday — it's gone!" One woman in the class stared at me with the strangest look, and I could guess what she was thinking. But before I could say it myself, another class member spoke out: "You know Kevin didn't heal her. That was the Lord's doing. He would tell you that himself."

So to add to that I simply said, "We all laid hands on her and prayed. We know that the Lord healed her." I insisted that Thelma keep the ophthalmology appointment. The following Sunday she told us that the ophthalmologist confirmed there was nothing wrong with the eye.

In Colossians 3:17 (NASB), it says: "Whatever you do in word or deed, do all in the name of the Lord Jesus, giving thanks through Him to God the Father." And we read in Hebrews 13:20-21 (NLT), "May the God of peace…equip you with all you need for doing his will. May he produce in you, through the power of Jesus Christ, every good thing that is pleasing to him."

Kevin Schoeppel

ELEVEN
Reasons to Believe

What are the reasons behind the things in which we believe? Even if you are a medium or a psychic yourself, you must admit that validation — that is, seeing the physical proof that the information you received in your mind or from a spirit is true — is important for someone to believe in your messages, or even for *you* to believe and have confidence in yourself. And to someone like me, who is neither a psychic nor a medium, these proofs of messages from psychics and mediums are equally important. The more that messages from psychics or mediums are proven to be correct, the more trust I can put into acting upon them in the future.

Even though I do not ask for readings myself, I would not refuse a message from anyone who had a message they felt compelled to share with me. The Bible only commands that I do not turn to persons with familiar spirits for guidance, but rather to trust in the Lord. And so knowing many psychics and mediums, I do occasionally receive psychically-obtained messages from them. And no matter how well or how long I have known the psychic or medium, I still look forward to seeing those messages come true. And no matter how many times I have seen it before, there is something quite awe-inspiring to see the validation of their messages unfold. It is evidence of Spirit in our lives.

Trust in a psychic or medium isn't just about their information coming true, but about the quality of that information as well. It is similar to the way a banker would review a loan application. He or she looks for some sort of track record of income and loan history for good reason to believe that a new loan will be repaid in full with interest. But instead of looking for money and payments, we are looking for accurate fulfillment of psychic messages. So as a gauge for trusting a psychic or medium, we can look at several things:

1. How often and how many times in the past has the psychic or medium been correct?

2. How specific or detailed was their information?

3. How many of those details turned out to be correct versus not correct?

4. Is there a reasonable way the psychic or medium could have received the information in a normal sensory manner?

5. How high would the odds probably be against the psychic's information being correct?

6. Could the outcome reasonably have been "rigged," or set up to be fulfilled?

Let's take an example from Scripture and apply these tests. In Mark 14:12-16 (NLT), Jesus gives two of his disciples specific commands about how they will find the right place to celebrate Passover: "On the first day of the Festival of Unleavened Bread, when the Passover lamb is sacrificed, Jesus' disciples asked him, 'Where do you want us to go to prepare the Passover meal for you?'

"So Jesus sent two of his disciples into Jerusalem with these instructions: 'As you go into the city, a man carrying a pitcher of water will meet you. Follow him. At the house he enters, say to the owner, 'The Teacher asks: Where is the guest room where I can eat the Passover meal with my disciples?' He will take you upstairs to

Kevin Schoeppel

a large room that is already set up. That is where you should prepare our meal.' So the two disciples went into the city and found everything just as Jesus had said, and they prepared the Passover meal there."

Jesus had already at this point had his past predictions and information proven right. And Jesus' information was very specific. We don't know how common it was back then to walk into a city and meet up with a man carrying a pitcher of water, but Jesus did not just say that it would be "a person" or even "someone working." The man could have chosen to try to lose these disciples of Jesus, who were following him, but he let them continue to follow him. In a city, "the house he enters" could be hundreds or thousands of possible homes. But this man goes into a house that just happens to have a large, upstairs room, already set up. The owner of the house lets them use the room. Again, Jesus could have just said "a room" or "some place" or even said they might have had to prepare it themselves.

It took trust in Jesus for his disciples to approach the owner of the house — likely a complete stranger — and say what they were told to say. The owner could have said, "Just who is this 'Teacher?' I don't even know who *you* are! Who does he think he is, just sending you in here expecting me to let you use my house? *Get out of here!*" Yes, it could have ended like that, but it did not. The Bible says that the disciples "found everything just as Jesus had said." Just meeting the man with the water pitcher — not so likely to have happened by chance — may have been enough to convince the two disciples that the rest of the details would happen too.

As well, Jesus really had no reasonable way to have known all of this non-supernaturally, and it wouldn't have been reasonable for him to "rig it up" to come true. He had no way to call ahead and arrange it so the man with the water pitcher would be waiting to take the disciples to exactly a place that Jesus had reserved ahead of time. It would have been more ridiculous — and a bigger waste of Jesus' time — to set up a hoax than to simply make all of the arrangements himself. By now Jesus had performed enough miracles and said enough things that had come true, that he didn't need to go to silly extremes to stage all of this so his disciples would believe in him.

A more contemporary example of this test is Tami's prediction of the football game that neither team won. It would be unreasonable to imagine her asking the football teams of both Rincon and Palo Verde High Schools: "Can you guys fix it so that the game ends in a tie? I've got a boyfriend I want to impress by letting him think I'm psychic."

When Stanna told our new friend, the massage therapist, exactly what song she had been listening to when she had drawn a pencil-sketch of a dragon — can you imagine how many songs per year are released in *each genre of music*? This makes the odds against Stanna being correct regarding one particular song, thousands — or perhaps *millions* — to one.

So it doesn't take a math genius to see that the odds against all of Jesus' instructions randomly happening to being correct, one event after another, had to be at least thousands to one against it all happening exactly as he said it would happen. Just for the man with the water pitcher to lead the disciples to exactly the right house in a city full of dwellings would tell you this, even before really figuring in the odds of the other details.

Jesus had already proven to his disciples, and to others, that he supernaturally knew things many times before in his ministry. Sometimes it would be private information of the past or present that would astonish the listener. Other times it would be a prediction that would come true shortly thereafter.

The Lord knows that for our hearts to be turned to Him, we *need* to see the supernatural and to be amazed by it. Without seeing these miraculous, unexplainable things happening in our lives, we only "pay lip service" to God, and serving him won't come from the heart. The Lord says: "These people say they are mine. They honor me with their lips, but their hearts are far from me. And their worship of me is nothing but man-made rules learned by rote." (Isaiah 29:13, NLT) But then he adds: *"Because of this, I will once again astound these hypocrites with amazing wonders. The wisdom of the wise will pass away, and the intelligence of the intelligent will disappear."* (Verse 14)

Have you ever been to a church service that just seems to be a ritualistic, robotic routine of the members who perhaps believe that *they have to be in church* to go to Heaven? God doesn't care for these boring rituals, or get any more pleasure from them, than the ones who are presenting them.

And the cure for this boring, meaningless, ritual type of worship isn't a more entertaining type of church service. God says: "How I wish one of you would shut the Temple doors so that these worthless sacrifices could not be offered! I am not pleased with you," says the Lord of Heaven's Armies, "and I will not accept your offerings!" (Malachi 1:10, NLT)

Each writer of the Gospels — Matthew, Mark, Luke, and John — wrote their story of Jesus from a different perspective. The apostle John wrote his so that we may see that Jesus was not just a teacher or prophet, but that he was actually the son of God (John 20:37). And in nearly every chapter of his book, John gives an example of a time Jesus validated who he was. Here are some examples: In John 1:48-50 (NLT), Philip, who had become a disciple, brings Nathaniel to Jesus, and Jesus says to him: "Now here is a genuine son of Israel — a man of complete integrity."

"How do you know about me?" Nathanael asked.

Jesus replied, "I could see you under the fig tree before Philip found you."

Then Nathanael exclaimed, "Rabbi, you are the Son of God — the King of Israel!"

Jesus asked him, "Do you believe this just because I told you I had seen you under the fig tree? You will see greater things than this!"

The Bible doesn't say what makes Jesus' statement significant to Nathaniel. My guess is that Nathaniel's favorite spot — the fig tree — was probably secluded. Maybe it was his private prayer spot. But there was something about Jesus saying that he saw him there that Nathaniel believed was quite out of the ordinary — so much so as to convince him that Jesus had supernatural abilities.

In John 2:7-10, Jesus was at a wedding feast in Cana that ran out of wine. He asked a group of servants to fill some stone jars with water, and then take some of it to the master of the feast. But after a taste, the master of the feast tells them that they had kept the best wine for last. Jesus hadn't done any trickery, and these servants knew it. They were the only ones that had handled the water before taking it to the master. They didn't know even when, or where, or how the water had turned to wine. And even though they might have felt silly going to the master of the feast with what they thought was just a drink of water, they chose to obey Jesus.

In John 4, Jesus went through Samaria and met a woman at a well. He asked her for a drink, and they talked. She told him nothing about her personal life. Jesus asked her to call for her husband. When she admitted that she had no husband, Jesus told her that she has spoken truthfully, and he went on to tell her that she has had five husbands, and that the man she was living with presently was not her husband. She was so amazed at his knowledge of her personal life that he couldn't possibly have known previously — for he had just met her there at the well — that she left her water pot, went into the city, and told everyone about the man who told her "everything she ever did." She asked, "Could this be the Christ?" Although Jesus had told the woman [in John 4:26], plainly, that he *was* the Christ, it was her amazement at his knowledge of the details of her life that made her really believe.

In John 10:17-18 (NASB), Jesus predicts his own death and resurrection. He says, "For this reason the Father loves Me, because I lay down My life so that I may take it again. No one has taken it away from Me, but I lay it down on My own initiative. I have authority to lay it down, and I have authority to take it up again. This commandment I received from My Father." It is amazing enough that Jesus actually rose bodily from the dead — *but even more amazing that he also predicted it in advance.*

But in John, chapter 11, Jesus does something even more amazing. After getting news that his friend Lazarus was sick, Jesus waits two more days before starting out for Bethany, where Lazarus lived. In fact, *he waits until Lazarus is dead* — and deliberately times it so that when Jesus and his disciples arrive in Bethany at the home of Mary and Martha it would be four days after their brother Lazarus died. Jesus tells Martha, Lazarus' sister: "Your brother will rise again." (John 11:23, NASB)

She replies in verse 24: "I know that he will rise again in the resurrection on the last day." She was merely repeating back a teaching that Jesus had said to her before. (John 6:40) And that is all she thinks Jesus is referring to when he told her that her brother would rise again. At that point Martha does not believe, nor is she even thinking, that Jesus will *physically* raise her brother up from the dead, and immediately so. Even the mourners apparently are thinking the same as Martha, because they say in verse 37: "Could not this man, who opened the eyes of the blind man, have kept this man also from dying?"

By this time in Jesus' ministry, the word had spread throughout the whole region about two other people that He had raised from the dead. So why didn't they have any faith now that he could do the same thing as before? In the case of the two other persons Jesus had raised from the dead — the son of the widow from Nain (Luke 7:11-17), and the daughter of Jairus, the synagogue leader (Mark 5:35-43) — each had been raised back to life within a few hours after they died, for it was a Jewish custom to bury the dead before sunset on the day of death. This, however, was not the case with Lazarus.

In pre-Christian times, the Zoroastrians taught that the spirit of a deceased person would remain near the body for about three days before moving on. The Jews, who had been in exile in Babylon and Persia during the sixth century, B.C., probably adopted this afterlife belief from them: "The greatest degree of mourning is in the first three days. The body is still intact and the soul hovers around it with the intention to return. When after three days it sees the face has changed and the person is no more, it starts to go away." (Genesis Rabba, chapter 100, verse 7)

Far from being merely an ancient Jewish belief, I have discovered this to be a fairly common presupposition among others as well — nursing home workers in particular — who have related to me their observations of unexplained phenomena, such as lights and electronic devices turning on and off by themselves, for up to three days following the passing of one of their former residents.

Lazarus, however, had now been dead *four* days. According to this Zoroastrian/Jewish belief, his spirit had to have already passed on and gone away, making any chance of a bodily resurrection seem impossible. And so Jesus prayed: "Father, I thank you that you have heard me. I knew that you always hear me; but because of the people standing around I said it, so that they may believe that you sent me." When He had said these things, He cried out with a loud voice, "Lazarus, come forth." The man who had died came forth, bound hand and foot with wrappings, and his face was wrapped around with a cloth. Jesus said to them, "Unbind him, and let him go." (John 11:41-44, NASB)

The other validations might have simply proved that Jesus was a gifted psychic. But by *this* validation, he was proving that he had *power over death and life* — something very necessary for us to know, if we are to trust him to be our Lord and Savior.

Jesus wasn't subject to any of the beliefs and principles of the afterlife. He said, "I AM the resurrection and the life." (John 11:25, KJV) *He created it and ruled over it.* By rising bodily from the dead himself, he not only fulfilled his own prediction, but those of the *Old Testament* prophets who had written about him. As Jesus himself said, "Thus it is written, that the Christ would suffer and rise again from the dead the third day." (Luke 24:46, NASB)

Today, many churches want you to make your beliefs in the Lord a matter of faith alone. But if you were to walk into those same churches and claim to have messages from spirits, or have psychic abilities, would they not expect to see some proof for what you are claiming?

Likewise, the Lord provides validation to the world of those who serve him. The signs, wonders, and miracles were the mark of an apostle, as Paul said, but he gives many other spiritual gifts to' prove to the world that He has sent you to serve Him. It is so that "your faith should not stand in the wisdom of men, but in the power of God." (1 Corinthians 2:5, KJV)

TWELVE
The Foundation of This Book: The Bible

Everything that you have read in this book is supported by the Bible. But why have I chosen the Bible as my authority, and not some other religion's book? What makes the Bible God's Word? Moreover, why should it matter whether The Bible is God's Word or not, as it pertains to your spiritual gift?

I have yet to find an atheist among the spiritually gifted — and this appears to be especially true of psychics and mediums. Every psychically gifted person I have ever known seems to recognize the existence of a higher power or a supreme being as the source of their gift.

Deep down inside, for many of them, it is *God*, and not simply a "higher power." The reason many of them hesitate in acknowledging God is because of the rejection they have experienced at the hands of Christians, or the Church, whom they have associated with God.

If you are a psychic or a medium, the very fact that you picked up this book tells me that you are concerned with God's acceptance of you. If you really didn't believe in God, but merely some "higher power" or "the Universe," you would not have felt compelled to read it, for any other reason than to hope to learn that God accepts you and loves you just as you are.

Many years ago, when that youth leader told me that a person who had an ability to know things before they happened was not from God, it was the start of my questioning why I believed what I

Kevin Schoeppel

believed. Was the Bible *really* the Word of God, or had I just been raised to believe that?

Along the way to finding my answers to those questions, a Christian apologetics speaker, Josh McDowell, initially provided me with his reasoning to trust that the Bible was really God's Word. But I had to do more research on my own to be fully convinced. Many years afterward, I taught what I had learned to my discipleship class, because members of that class did not really know how to answer people who might say to them, "The Bible is just a book of fantasy stories," or, "The Bible is just written by men like me and you, so how can we say it is different from any other religion's book?" Still other people would tell them that the Bible is full of contradictions, or that the Catholic Church changed the Bible to say what they wanted it to say in order to give more authority to their leadership. It is equally important now for you to understand that there are good reasons to trust that the Bible really is God's Word, particularly when someone makes statements like those.

There is no absolute proof that the Bible is definitely God's Word, nor can I point to conclusive proof that the other religion's writings are *not* God's Word. So what should we be looking for in order to convince us *beyond a reasonable doubt* that the Bible is the Word of God?

A book written by God, and not just men, should have supernatural characteristics as a mark of authorship by Him. Like the workings of the spiritual gifts that are written about in the Bible, these characteristics should demonstrate a vast difference between what God could write and what ordinary men could write.

In the early twentieth century, Arthur W. Pink wrote in *The Divine Inspiration of the Bible:*

"If the Bible be the Word of God, then it infinitely transcends in value all the writings of men. . .it stands on an infinitely exalted plane, all alone; if it immeasurably transcends all the greatest productions of human genius; then, we should naturally expect to find that it has unique credentials, that there are internal marks which prove it to be the handiwork of God."

Here are those unique credentials that I discovered about the Bible, which sets it in a class by itself, far above all other written works of the ancient world, both religious and secular:

1. **The Bible is unique in its continuity.** 40 authors over 16 centuries in such diverse places as Rome, Egypt, Greece, Jerusalem, Persia and Babylon are harmoniously complementary in writing God's plan of redemption of mankind.

2. **The Bible is unique in its circulation**. Approximately 700 million copies of the Bible are printed and circulated every year. The second-place book, *The Guinness Book of World Records*, took 48 years to sell 100 million copies.

3. **The Bible is unique in its translation.** It was translated into 5 languages by 300 A.D. when it was unheard of to translate any book at all, and today is translated into over 2,400 languages. *The Guinness Book of World Records*, by comparison, has been translated into 37 languages.

4. **The Bible is unique in its survival** when compared with other ancient manuscripts. Over 5,300 manuscripts of

the New Testament survive, with less than a 0.25% textual discrepancy which has easily been 100% resolved in such a large group of manuscripts. Even though Muslims, for example, claim that the Koran has been handed down intact since Mohammad, this is widely disputed — as you will discover by putting the words "textual," "accuracy," and "Koran" into any Internet search engine and reading the search results.

5. **The Bible is unique in its authenticity.** There are no original manuscripts which exist of *any* ancient book, including the Bible. However, the earliest existing *copies* of the *New Testament* date back to within fifty to one-hundred years of the time of the original manuscripts. By contrast, the earliest existing copies of non-Biblical documents from that era of history date back no earlier than eight-hundred years after the original manuscripts were written. The shorter the time from the original to its earliest surviving copy, the greater are the chances of its faithfulness to the original work.

6. **The Bible is inerrant.** All apparent discrepancies have been found to be complementary accounts, failure to compare contexts and related scripture, or translation wording differences.

7. **The Bible is unique in its prophecy.** No other major established religious book includes prophecy, much less detailed prophecies that have held true, including prophecies of Israel that have been fulfilled in just the last century. You can demonstrate this to yourself by putting "prophecy" and "-Bible" (the minus sign before the word "Bible" means "must *not* contain the

word 'Bible'") into any Internet search engine. You may find search results like *The Celestine Prophecy*, but no results that discuss prophecy being in any other religion's holy books.

8. **The Bible's canonization** was not decided by groups or councils, but by the entire body of followers of Christ, over a period of three centuries of common acceptance by those followers.

9. **The Bible is unique in its influence** of our laws, morals, language, names, phrases, works of art, films, and music to an extent that no other book even comes close to doing. *By itself*, with no human intervention, it has led men to salvation by repentance and belief in the Lord Jesus Christ.

10. **And finally, the Bible accomplished all** of the above and remains relevant in spite of twenty centuries of efforts from kings, countries, political movements, and social organizations to eradicate it from the face of the Earth.

These facts are astounding enough to stand on their own as compelling evidence that the Bible far outstrips all secular literature ever written. These facts are also useable in making comparisons with documents that attempt to refute the historical facts that are in the Bible.

Whenever you might read books and articles that refer to documentary evidence attempting to refute the historical accuracy of the Bible, ask yourself: *How do we know that document (the one opposing the Bible) has been handed down correctly throughout the ages? How many copies of it are in existence? How many textual discrepancies are in it? How many years' difference*

is there between the original writing and its oldest existing copy?
Once you make a one-on-one comparison of the other ancient
document's credentials again those of the Bible's, its arguments
weaken considerably.

Still, astounding as these facts are in and of themselves, they don't
address the issue of whether there is any indication that *God* wrote
the Bible, or if *men* wrote the Bible. The apostle Peter states in 1
Peter 1:20-21 (NASB): "No prophecy of Scripture is a matter of
one's own interpretation, for no prophecy was ever made by an act
of human will, but men moved by the Holy Spirit spoke from
God."

And it appears that the other writers of the Bible had the same
impression of their work as Peter did. John Urquhart, in his 1895
book, *The Inspiration and Accuracy of the Holy Scriptures* writes:

> "The actual writers of these scriptures — the Law,
> the Psalms and the Prophets, the Gospels and the
> Epistles, and the Revelation — must also have
> been convinced that they were writing not their
> own words but the words of God Himself. In fact
> they say so themselves. And this [consistent view
> of having written the words of God] was
> maintained in one set of writings for fifteen-
> hundred years, from Moses to the apostle John,
> and is found in no other set of writings anywhere
> in the world.

> But this view of their own words is most unusual.
> Men do not willingly ascribe the authority of their
> words, and especially of their ideas, to someone
> else. They are only too eager to claim the credit
> for what they write. How then could this unique

attitude have been preserved without wavering by the writers of the Bible? There is only one reasonable explanation: There was a "Mind" behind it all, directing what was written and taught. No men of themselves could have maintained this most unnatural view of their own work consistently over so many centuries."

Although Peter was referring to the *Old Testament* when he said that Scripture was "men being moved by the Holy Spirit," this had to apply to him, too. Peter didn't actually have a style of writing of his own. In fact, he had no formal education. In Acts 4:13 (HCSB), we read that: "When they (*the family of the High Priest, from verse 6*), observed the boldness of Peter and John and realized that they were uneducated and untrained men, they were amazed and recognized that they had been with Jesus." When he wrote First Peter, he said: "I have written and sent this short letter to you with the help of Silas." (1 Peter 5:12, NLT)

And yet, the writings of this uneducated fisherman from the Sea of Galilee have stood the test of time far better than the literature of the highly educated people of his day. Why is this so? What did his writing have that his contemporaries' writings didn't? Urquhart offers the answer: Peter was but one of many persons who was a human instrument of what Urquhart called the "Mind behind it all," directing what was written.

Arthur W. Pink's words in his 1917 book, *The Divine Inspiration of the Bible*, complement those of Urquhart, but they add a different perspective worth considering:

"The Bible was penned on two continents, written in three languages, and its composition and compilation extended through the slow progress of sixteen centuries. The various parts of the Bible were written at different times and under the most varying circumstances. Parts of it were written in tents, deserts, cities, palaces and dungeons; in times of imminent danger and in seasons of ecstatic joy.

Among its writers were judges, kings, priests, prophets, patriarchs, prime ministers, herdsmen, scribes, soldiers, physicians and fishermen. Yet despite these varying circumstances, conditions and workmen, the Bible is one Book, behind its many parts there is an unmistakable organic unity. It contains one system of doctrine, one code of ethics, one plan of salvation and one rule of faith.

Human writers reflect the spirit of their own day and generation and the compositions of men living amid widely differing influences and separated by centuries of time have little or nothing in common with each other. Yet. . . we find a perfect harmony throughout the Scriptures from the first verse in Genesis to the last verse in Revelation.

The great ethical and spiritual lessons presented in the Bible, by whoever taught, agree. The more one really studies the Bible, the more one is convinced that behind the many human mouths there is one overruling, controlling Mind."

If this "one overruling, controlling Mind" is indeed the Almighty God, He can foretell the future. And the most unique quality of the Bible which sets it apart from all other human literature, and the holy books of other faiths, is its prophecies.

It would seem easy to dismiss *Old Testament* prophecy being fulfilled in the *New Testament* as one being written to fit the other. So let's look at an example of a highly improbable *Old Testament* prophecy that was fulfilled about twenty-six hundred years after it was written, and over sixteen hundred years after the Scriptures — both the *Old Testament* and *New Testament*, as we know them — were completed.

In Jeremiah 23:7-8 (NLT), the Bible tells us that the Lord says: "In that day, when people are taking an oath, they will no longer say, 'As surely as the Lord lives, who rescued the people of Israel from the land of Egypt.' Instead, they will say, 'As surely as the Lord lives, who brought the people of Israel back to their own land from the land of the north and from all the countries to which he had exiled them.' Then they will live in their own land."

By examining the verses preceding this prophecy, it appears that the Lord was not talking about the return of the Israelites from the nation of Babylon — but returning to a sovereign nation of their own. At that time of the return from Babylon they were only a province of Persia, and in Jesus' time they were a province of Rome. After the destruction of Jerusalem in 70 AD, the Jews remaining in Palestine were scattered all over the world, and had no place in the world to call their home.

The 1917 edition of the *Scofield Reference Bible* contains this study note to these verses: "The restoration here foretold [of a nation of Israel] is not to be confounded with the return of a feeble remnant of Judah under Ezra, Nehemiah, and Zerubbabel at the end of the 70 years (Jeremiah 29:10). . .This prophecy is yet to be fulfilled."

In 1948, Israel became a sovereign nation again in their original homeland. And now more than sixty years after that, Israel continues to retain their homeland. No other nation, ancient or modern, has ever accomplished such a feat. What are the odds against it? Who knows? Yet the Bible foretold it and it came to pass.

So you now see that there are many compelling reasons to believe that the Bible is the Word of God — its unique characteristics which far exceed those of other literature, the evidence of one controlling mind guiding sixteen centuries of authorship, and its prophecies — both those already fulfilled, and those *yet to be fulfilled.*

THIRTEEN
Departure of the Disciples:
Why No New Scripture?

You may have already been surprised at some of the things which
you have read in this book. If you were raised by your family to go
to church, as I was, you may have even wondered why, if all of
these teachings are supported by the Bible — the same Bible that
your church taught, the same Bible that they claim (and that I
purport, too) is the Word of God — that you were not taught some
of these things which you have read here.

Or conversely, why you were taught things by your church that
you *thought* were in the Bible, only to find out later that the Bible
does not support that teaching — for example, the belief that a
believer in Christ is in Heaven when they die. The "surprise" is
probably due to you finding out that what your *church taught* was
different from what the *Bible taught* — not the other way around!
The Bible didn't change.

Jesus said almost two-thousand years ago, "Heaven and earth shall
pass away, but my words shall not pass away." (Matthew 24:35,
KJV) He also said, "I tell you the truth, until heaven and earth
disappear, not even the smallest detail of God's law will disappear
until its purpose is achieved." (Matthew 5:18, NLT)

What does having a Bible that does not change have to do with
spiritual gifts, particularly psychic and mediumship abilities?
Many of you may have encountered a person or persons who have
stated that the Bible says mediums are in contact with demonic
spirits, and that psychic abilities come from being involved in the

occult. Of course, you know now that neither of these statements is true, because they cannot be Biblically proven. But if God's Word *could* be changed, then what I have written in this book would alert the religious leaders of the world to "a need to amend the Bible." Then, after they "closed the loophole," *any* psychic or medium would have no hope for the future — only the fear and dread of an impending eternity in the Lake of Fire, separated from God's love, forever.

Near the end of the first century, the apostles — those persons who had walked with Jesus and learned from Jesus firsthand as his disciples — were concerned about preserving and protecting his teachings from being corrupted after their passing. They wanted to preserve his teachings in writing, and to entrust the passing on of those teachings to reliable, trusted men.

Jesus said that his words will never pass away (see Mark 13:31), and the evidence of the Bible's survival shows that this is being fulfilled. But when we leave it up to men to teach us what those writings say, corruption inevitably happens. We get truth when we read Scripture for ourselves. And this was the intention behind the apostles' task of preserving Jesus' teachings by written Scripture.

+ + + + +

In pursuing their goal of preserving the truth in writing, the apostles may have been thinking about what happened in the days of King Josiah in the *Old Testament*. In 2 Chronicles 34:8-33, the king had ordered the repair of the temple of the Lord. Hilkiah, the high priest, found a copy of the Scriptures in the temple, which the king's secretary read to him. When the king heard what the actual Scriptures taught, he tore his robes in sorrow to find out that the people of Israel had not been keeping the teaching of the Scriptures.

And it was only about two hundred years after King Josiah's time that the Lord said to the people through the prophet Malachi: "For the lips of a priest should preserve knowledge, and men should seek instruction from his mouth; for he is the messenger of the Lord of hosts. But as for you, you have turned aside from the way; you have caused many to stumble by the instruction." says the Lord of hosts." (Malachi 2:7-8, NASB).

If corruption of spiritual teachings could happen at least twice — just in the history that the apostles could read about in the *Old Testament* — it could certainly happen again — and has, even today.

The apostle, Paul, told the leaders of the church at Ephesus: "I know that false teachers, like vicious wolves, will come in among you after I leave, not sparing the flock. Even some men from your own group will rise up and distort the truth in order to draw a following. Watch out!" (Acts 20:29-31, NLT)

Jesus himself made the original "wolves in sheep's clothing" warning many years earlier: "Beware of false prophets who come disguised as harmless sheep but are really vicious wolves. You can identify them by their fruit, that is, by the way they act." (Matthew 7:15-16, NLT) This wasn't only for Jesus' time, or Paul's time. It still applies today.

Jesus told us: "Anyone who listens to my teaching and follows it is wise, like a person who builds a house on solid rock." (Matthew 7:24, NLT)

James 1:22 (KJV) says: "Be ye doers of the word, and not hearers only, deceiving yourselves." How could we be certain that we would have the *actual words* to put into practice, to make sure our spiritual foundations are solid as a rock? *This* was the challenge of the disciples still alive in the late first century.

Peter wrote: "There will be false teachers among you. They will cleverly teach destructive heresies and even deny the Master who bought them. In this way, they will bring sudden destruction on themselves. Many will follow their evil teaching and shameful immorality. And because of these teachers, the way of truth will be slandered. In their greed they will make up clever lies to get hold of your money. But God condemned them long ago, and their destruction will not be delayed." (2 Peter 2:1-3, NLT)

The apostle John wrote: "So you must remain faithful to what you have been taught from the beginning. If you do, you will remain in fellowship with the Son and with the Father. And in this fellowship we enjoy the eternal life he promised us. I am writing these things to warn you about those who want to lead you astray. But you have received the Holy Spirit, and he lives within you, so you don't need anyone to teach you what is true. For the Spirit teaches you everything you need to know, and what he teaches is true — it is not a lie. So, just as he has taught you, remain in fellowship with Christ." (1 John 2:24-27, NLT)

Jesus, Peter, Paul, and John all were aware that once they were no longer in this world, leaders would arise who would distort the truth. Why would these leaders want to distort God's Word? Peter gave us one reason: Greed. Jesus gave us several more: Control, status, attention, and power.

In Matthew 23:4-7 (NLT), in talking about the Pharisees, who were considered the religious leaders amongst the Jews, Jesus said: "They crush people with unbearable religious demands and never lift a finger to ease the burden. Everything they do is for show. On their arms they wear extra wide prayer boxes with Scripture verses inside, and they wear robes with extra long tassels. And they love to sit at the head table at banquets and in the seats of honor in the synagogues. They love to receive respectful greetings as they walk in the marketplaces, and to be called 'Rabbi.'"

Even within their own lifetime, the apostles had already observed how the Pharisees had been distorting the truth of the *Old Testament* Scriptures. In Mark 7:9-13 (NLT), Jesus tells them: "You skillfully sidestep God's law in order to hold on to your own tradition. For instance, Moses gave you this law from God: 'Honor your father and mother,' and 'Anyone who speaks disrespectfully of father or mother must be put to death.' But you say it is alright for people to say to their parents, 'Sorry, I can't help you, for I have vowed to give to God what I would have given to you.' In this way, you let them disregard their needy parents. And so you cancel the word of God in order to hand down your own tradition. And this is only one example among many others."

The religious leaders had not changed the actual *Old Testament* Scriptures, but were *adding* traditions and regulations that they were teaching as equivalent in authority to Scripture. Jesus is saying here that any traditions *must not* set aside, or nullify, the words and commands of Scripture.

All *New Testament* books were either written by (or someone close to), a person who had known the Lord Jesus Christ personally during His time on Earth. And first-hand authorship is one of the essential requirements for these books to be considered authoritative, or *canonical*. While there were other standards that books of the *New Testament* had to meet in order to be canonical, this requirement — knowing Jesus first-hand — ensured that there would be a permanent, fixed authority that all future believers could rely upon. Once these writers were no longer alive, no future writings could possibly meet this same requirement.

You may be asking at this point, "Why all this concern about preserving the teachings? Couldn't the apostles appear at any time to mediums who serve the Lord, critiquing the church's teachings, praising those who are standing firm in the truth, and condemning those who have led people astray?" No. And there are several reasons why not.

First, not all persons are mediums. Not all persons who follow Jesus' teachings are mediums, either. On the other hand, *anyone* can become a follower of Christ. "Those the Father has given me will come to me, and I will never reject them." (John 6:37, NLT)

Second, if God had planned for the disciples to continue revealing truth from the other side through mediums, instead of through the Bible, there would be a natural division between the followers of Jesus, There would be the mediums, those who would have a direct connection to the truth. And there would be non-mediums, who would be dependent upon the mediums for the truth.

Third, even a medium gifted by God is only human, and any follower of Christ can be tempted by ego, pride, greed, status, and the desire for power. Apostolic guidance through mediums has the same inherent problems associated with false teachers. The non-medium might, for status reasons, attempt to "become" a medium and fall victim to disobeying God in the process, because he or she would be then be practicing to contact familiar spirits.

Not only does such a person have no part in ministry (as Peter told Simon the sorcerer in Acts 8:21), but God never intended for there to be division among his people: "Make every effort to keep yourselves united in the Spirit, binding yourselves together with peace. For there is one body and one Spirit, just as you have been called to one glorious hope for the future. There is one Lord, one faith, one baptism." (Ephesians 4:3-5, NLT)

And the final reason is that even messages to God-gifted mediums aren't foolproof either, especially if the medium were to fail to test the spirits as the Bible commands.

Since it was God's intent to bring all persons together equally under Christ Jesus, then all persons would need equal access to what God wants them to know. If a non-medium follower wanted to know what information he needed to know to follow Jesus, and did not know of any mediums, would he be at a disadvantage if he only had access to the standard, sixty-six book canonical Bible as we know it? The answer is "No."

"All scripture is given by inspiration of God, and is profitable for doctrine, for reproof, for correction, for instruction in righteousness, that the man of God may be perfect, thoroughly furnished unto all good works." (2 Timothy 3:16-17, KJV) Yes, "thoroughly furnished" with all he needs — and without any need for "revision." Hebrews 13:8 (KJV) says: "Jesus Christ is the same yesterday, today and forever." If Jesus does not change, then the *New Testament* as the apostles recorded it does not require amending.

An authoritative line needed to be drawn by the early Christian church, to distinguish the writings of those who had personally known Jesus, from the writings of those who had not. And that had to be done while those who had personally known those writers still lived.

Have you ever read a book, article, or even a letter which claimed to have been written by someone you knew, but the wording "just didn't sound like them?" and later your suspicions were confirmed?

Or conversely, did you ever have an assignment to write a paper for an English class when you were in high school or college, but needed help in writing it, and so had someone else write it for you? Chances are that your teacher always somehow knew you had the "help," because the writing style was different than if you had written it.

The same would be true of the writers of the *New Testament*. There is a difference in the writing about the teachings of Jesus by those who personally knew Him, versus those who had not. For example, some Gnostic texts such as the "Gospel of Mary" or "Gospel of Thomas" were ultimately excluded from the *New Testament* because of persons in the first-century church who had known the real Thomas and the real Mary, and knew that these books were not genuinely written by them.

Knowing that in the future there would still exist mediums, or persons with the gift of prophecy, these *New Testament* books by persons who personally knew Jesus are the standard by which any future message claiming to be from the Lord could be determined to be authentic or not. New messages from Spirit can supplement, but should never be equal to, nor override, the canonized Scriptures.

The Bereans in Paul's time applied this test of authenticity by comparing any purported message from God to the standard of the *Old Testament*. They "listened eagerly" to Paul's message. They "searched the Scriptures day after day to see if Paul and Silas were teaching the truth." (See Acts 17:11, NLT)

The Bible even intended itself to be a test for a medium or psychic's message. Isaiah 8:19-20 (NASB) says in part: "When they say to you, "Consult the mediums and the spiritists . . . if they do not speak according to this word, it is because they have no dawn."

FOURTEEN
The Most Important of All

Imagine that you are at the end of time. You are standing before the Lord Jesus Christ. Either the kingdom of Heaven awaits you, or the Lake of Fire awaits you. You basically lived a good life and you used your spiritual gifts to benefit others. You did your deeds in the name of the Lord to bring glory to Him. And then he speaks: "I never knew you. Get away from me."

I'm not making this up. Far from it being just a possibility, Jesus said this will actually happen to many persons. He tells us in Matthew 7:21-23 (NLT): "Not everyone who calls out to me, 'Lord! Lord!' will enter the Kingdom of Heaven. Only those who actually do the will of my Father in heaven will enter. On judgment day many will say to me, 'Lord! Lord! We prophesied in your name and cast out demons in your name and performed many miracles in your name.' But I will reply, 'I never knew you. Get away from me, you who break God's laws.'"

What could have gone wrong? How could people who did all of these supernatural things —prophesying, performing miracles, and casting out demons, especially those saying they did them in Jesus' name — be told, "I never knew you?" Wouldn't demonstrating such abilities mean that they belong to Jesus?

Strangely enough, no. Having these abilities, though, can deceive you into thinking that you belong to Christ, when in fact you do not. Having the Holy Spirit dwelling within you is quite a different thing from simply having the gifts of the Spirit. The Holy Spirit himself is our guarantee of a place in the Kingdom of Heaven, but having spiritual gifts is not. Spiritual gifts are not the evidence that the Holy Spirit is within you. The *fruit* of the Spirit, however — which manifests love, joy, peace, patience, kindness, goodness, faithfulness, gentleness, and self-control — *is* evidence that He is within you, and at work in your spiritual growth.

Since I do not want you to be one of those who gets this rejection from Jesus at the judgment, I will show you from the Bible what we all need to do to make certain that our final destination is the Kingdom of Heaven. And I will point out the errors that many people rely on to get there so that you will not make those same mistakes.

Why do I say "final destination?" Sheol, or Hades, is the *current* place where those who have passed reside. These are simply the Hebrew and Greek names, respectively, for "the place of the dead." Many persons believe that "Hades" is synonymous for "Hell." But Sheol or Hades does *not mean* "Hell." Spirits who contact mediums presently are in this "place of the dead." This place of the dead has many "compartments" (as I am told by mediums), some of which are named in Scripture. Psychics and mediums commonly refer to this place as "the other side," regardless of their faith, or *lack* of faith, in any god.

But these spirits will not remain in Hades forever. That place will be destroyed. When it is destroyed, the spirits there will face the Lord's judgment, along with those who are living at that time. The Bible tells us: "The sea gave up the dead which were in it, and death and Hades gave up the dead which were in them; and they were judged, every one of them according to their deeds. Then death and Hades were thrown into the lake of fire. This is the second death, the lake of fire." (Revelation 20:13-14, NASB)

How do we ensure that once "the other side" is destroyed, our home for the remainder of eternity is the Kingdom of Heaven and not the lake of fire?

First of all, Jesus said that the person who wants eternal life in the Kingdom of Heaven must do the will of his Father in Heaven. What is that? The five thousand people whom Jesus fed with five loaves of bread and two fish, asked him that in John 6:28-29 (NASB): "They said to Him, 'What shall we do, so that we may work the works of God?' Jesus answered and said to them, 'This is the work of God, that you believe in Him whom He has sent.'"

"Believing in him whom he has sent," is *not* just believing that Jesus is the son of God and that he actually exists. This is a grave mistake many people make — that if they believe in God, they will go to Heaven. But the Bible says: "You believe that there is one God. Good for you! Even the demons believe this, and they tremble in terror." (James 2:19, NLT) To really "believe in the one God has sent," we actually must believe *everything* about Him and understand how that relates to us. So first, we must believe — and confess — that Jesus Christ is Lord over our lives.

The Bible says in Romans 10:9-10 (NLT): "If you confess with your mouth that Jesus is Lord and believe in your heart that God raised him from the dead, you will be saved. For it is by believing in your heart that you are made right with God, and it is by confessing with your mouth that you are saved."

What does "Lord" actually mean? In *Webster's Revised Unabridged Dictionary* (1828), the first definition of the word "Lord" is: "1. A master; a person possessing supreme power and authority; a ruler; a governor."

Jesus said: "All authority has been given to me in heaven and on earth." (Matthew 28:18, NASB) If you believe in God, or Jesus Christ, but do not believe he has authority over you, then you really DON'T believe in him. This is why Jesus asked in Luke 6:46 (NASB): "Why do you call me, 'Lord, Lord,' and do not do what I say?"

How long would you last at your job if you do not do what your supervisor tells you to do? You can call him or her your supervisor, but if you don't follow his or her orders, you would be given a warning, and probably be fired the next time. And calling Jesus 'Lord' means, "Jesus, you are my supervisor, and I know that means I have to do what you tell me to do."

It is important for you to understand that obeying Jesus is *not* the same as obeying a pastor, a priest, or a church leader. This is a mistake that many people have been led to believe, and one which has led to frustration and rebellion against God, Jesus, the Bible, and the church. I have found that in reality, whenever I have listened to a person vent their frustrations about religion, church, or Christianity in particular, the source of their angst was actually caused by the words or actions of a pastor or church leader, *not* God, nor the Bible.

You are not required to obey a pastor or church leader as if they were Jesus. They do not have the authority over your life that Jesus has. Pastors and leaders have a responsibility to guide you in becoming acquainted with the Bible so that you may learn and know how to follow Jesus, but Jesus' commands for us are in the Bible. The Holy Spirit is your guide for understanding what you need to do with what you read in the Bible and how to put it into action for obeying Christ.

Jesus may also give you orders in visions and dreams, as He did with the Apostle Paul (see Acts 16:9-10 and Acts 27:23-24), but those orders will complement what he has already commanded for all of us in Scripture.

Jesus is our Lord. But we also must believe who He truly is. He is not merely a teacher, a prophet, or a highly spiritual person. The Bible says that Jesus is "the image of the invisible God, the firstborn of all creation. For by him all things were created, both in the heavens and on earth, visible and invisible, whether thrones or dominions or rulers or authorities—all things have been created through him and for him. He is before all things, and in him all things hold together. He is also head of the body, the church; and he is the beginning, the firstborn from the dead, so that he himself will come to have first place in everything. For it was the Father's good pleasure for all the fullness to dwell in him." (Colossians 1:15-19, NASB)

That's right. He is the almighty creator in the flesh and nothing less. If you do not believe this, you do not believe in him. It's true that Jesus obeys the Father, and that would seem to mean he is less than God. It is hard for us to understand that relationship and yet believe He is God in the flesh, but until we can understand this fully, we need to trust God's Word when it tells us: "For in Christ lives all the fullness of God in a human body." (Colossians 2:9, NLT) Don't expect to fully understand that, even in this lifetime. Some things are meant to be understood later, as the apostle Paul wrote: "All that I know now is partial and incomplete, but then I will know everything completely." (1 Corinthians 13:12, NLT)

The second thing we must do is repent. Repent? What is that? *Why do I have to do it?* Before I explain what "repenting" is, let's understand that *all* of us have done things that God's laws said not to do, or didn't do things that God said we must do. Don't believe for even a moment that we will be judged on the basis of whether our good deeds outweigh all of our bad deeds. Many people believe that is how we will be judged. But that way of thinking doesn't even hold up here with our earthly government and court system, let alone the judgment we will face before Christ.

To illustrate, let's imagine that you get a ticket for failure to obey a traffic law. Instead of paying the fine, you choose to go to court.

You explain to the judge that because you drive carefully and obey the law the other three hundred sixty four days of the year, he should dismiss the ticket because your good driving outweighs your bad driving.

Ridiculous? Wouldn't work? Right. But, strangely enough, many people make the very serious mistake of believing that God's judgment works that way. Living a good life *never* gets rid of any disobedience we have had previously in our lives. Any and all disobeying must be paid for, in the same way that our courts have fines, community service, probation, or jail time to pay for breaking our earthly laws.

Do you really think you might have kept all of God's commands? Let's take just one for example: "Children, obey your parents in the Lord, for this is right." (Ephesians 6:1, KJV) Can you remember *any time* while you were growing up that you disobeyed your parents? Then you have broken God's commands, just like the rest of us. And so a price must be paid.

However, Jesus Christ paid it for you when He shed his blood on the cross. All we need to do is accept the payment that He made. Romans 5:6-8 (NLT) tells us: "Christ came at just the right time and died for us sinners." Now, most people would not be willing to die for an upright person, although someone might perhaps be willing to die for a person who is especially good. But God showed his great love for us by sending Christ to die for us while we were still sinners.

If you have ever heard anyone use the logic that "a loving God wouldn't send anyone to Hell," they are overlooking the fact that He is also a *just* God, who must judge and sentence those who broke his laws. The difference is, God the Father sent Jesus — our Lord — to pay those sentences for us *because he IS a loving God,*

AND doesn't want to send anyone to Hell. But we must accept his payment of our sentence on *his* terms. And one of these terms is to repent. Jesus said, "Unless you repent, you will all likewise perish." (Luke 13:3, NASB)

Repenting is not apologizing. Repenting is:

- Turning away from the things that might cause us to disobey God; (Ezekiel 18:30)
- Getting rid of evil ways and thoughts; (Isaiah 55:7)
- Returning to the Lord with all of our heart; (Joel 2:12)
- Getting a new heart and a new spirit (Ezekiel 18:31)

Our "loving God" *commands* us to repent: "I have no pleasure in the death of anyone who dies," declares the Lord God. "Therefore, repent and live!" (Ezekiel 18:32, NASB)

Why repent? Repenting changes our thinking so we may serve the Lord. As an example of why this is necessary, consider the story of Simon in Acts 8:13-23. Simon was a sorcerer in the city of Samaria, who had amazed the people of Samaria with magic and had quite a following. However, when the apostle Philip came to Samaria, preaching the gospel along with signs and miracles performed by the power of the Holy Spirit, Simon believed in the Lord Jesus Christ and was baptized as a follower.

However, when he saw that the Holy Spirit was given by the laying on of the apostles' hands, he bribed Peter with money. Peter tells Simon, "May your silver perish with you, because you thought you could obtain the gift of God with money!. . .Your heart is not right before God." (Acts 8:20-21, NASB)

Without repenting, Simon's motives were all wrong. He believed in Jesus, but he wanted the power of the Holy Spirit so as to be able to amaze people as he had done before Philip had come to Samaria — *not* for the desire to serve the Lord with all of his heart.

If you have believed fully in the Lord Jesus Christ, and have repented, then you belong to Him. All other things that you do, such as baptism, are a result of following his commands as Lord of your life. You will not be rejected by God. Jesus said: "Those the Father has given me will come to me, and I will never reject them." (John 6:37, NLT)

But, as you recall, I went through a time of mistakenly thinking that God had rejected me, all because my earthly father had disinherited me. I had focused all of my thinking on what Jacob did to steal the blessing of his father that was intended for Esau, instead of realizing that Jesus had said He would never reject me. I should have considered this before making up my mind that God had rejected me.

You have already read that "God is not the author of confusion, but of peace." (1 Corinthians 14:33, KJV). So if I knew that I had believed and repented, which is all that Jesus said I must do to gain eternal life, why would I ever have become so narrow-minded in my thinking as to believe that God had rejected me? These kinds of thoughts come to us from our enemy to hinder our spiritual growth. "Be serious! Be alert! Your adversary the Devil is prowling around like a roaring lion, looking for anyone he can devour. Resist him and be firm in the faith." (1 Peter 5:8-9, HCSB) *That was what I had failed to do.*

While you were growing up, do you remember people who still tried to treat you like a little kid instead of recognizing that you had to mature and become an adult? You have spiritual opposition to your "growing up" in Christ, too. Paul said, "Who prevented you from obeying the truth? This persuasion did not come from the One who called you. Whoever it is that is confusing you will pay the penalty." (Galatians 5:7 and10, HCSB) As long as my thinking was confused, because I would only look at Scriptures that seemed to condemn me instead of looking at the whole truth of the Bible, I would not grow up spiritually to be able to lead others as I eventually did.

How do we make certain that we are His, and that we won't hear Him tell us at the end of time, "I never knew you?" This is important to understand. If we don't get this straight, we will never make the progress necessary to attain spiritual maturity.

First of all, the Spirit of the Lord will be in you, beginning from when you repent and decide to follow the Lord Jesus Christ by baptism. The Bible says: "Repent, and each of you be baptized in the name of Jesus Christ for the forgiveness of your sins; and you will receive the gift of the Holy Spirit." (Acts 2:38, NASB) He is your "seal," or guarantee, of salvation. 2 Corinthians 1:21-22, 2 Corinthians 5:5, and Ephesians 1:13-14 all say that receiving the Holy Spirit is a "deposit, guaranteeing what is to come."

Anyone who has ever bought a home knows what "earnest money" is — a deposit guaranteeing that the buyer will follow through with the purchase of the home. The Holy Spirit is God's guarantee that he will follow through with preparing a place for us in the Kingdom of Heaven.

Don't confuse having the Holy Spirit with having the *gifts* of the Holy Spirit. The Spirit himself is the Comforter, or Counselor, that Jesus promised to send to be with us forever. (See John 14:15, John 14:26, John 15:26, and John 16:7) His job is to convict us of sin, righteousness and judgment, to testify of Jesus, to teach us and guide us into all truth, remind us of all that Jesus has said, and give us understanding of God's Word. And, of course, he decides what spiritual gifts to give us.

The Bible says: "The Holy Spirit produces this kind of fruit in our lives: Love, joy, peace, patience, kindness, goodness, faithfulness, gentleness, and self-control." (Galatians 5:22-23, NLT) These things, as you continue to grow spiritually, will be your evidence that the Holy Spirit is guiding you and that you do have a heavenly dwelling.

The second way to confirm that we belong to Jesus is to check our thinking. Romans 8:5 (NASB) says: "Those who are according to the flesh set their minds on the things of the flesh, but those who are according to the Spirit, the things of the Spirit." What do you have your mind set on as you serve Christ? Philippians 2:5-7 (KJV) says: "Let this mind be in you, which was also in Christ Jesus: Who, being in the form of God, thought it not robbery to be equal with God: But made himself of no reputation, and took upon him the form of a servant."

This is the exact opposite of what Simon the Sorcerer's attitude was. He wanted to amaze people and to draw attention to himself. Jesus took on the form of a servant. In fact, Jesus told his disciples, "You know that those who are recognized as rulers of the Gentiles lord it over them; and their great men exercise authority over them. But it is not this way among you, but whoever wishes to become great among you shall be your servant; and whoever wishes to be first among you shall be slave of all. For even the Son of Man did not come to be served, but to serve, and to give His life a ransom for many." (Mark 10:42-45, NASB)

A third question you should ask yourself is: Do I have a desire to know and understand more of God's Word? The Bible says: "As newborn babes, desire the sincere milk of the word." (1 Peter 2:2, KJV) Over the years, I have watched litters of newborn puppies and kittens born in our home, and have seen how they latch on to their mother's nipple and won't stop nursing until they are full. It's part of their instinct as a newborn.

What makes a desire to understand the Bible a part of *our instinct?* Having the Holy Spirit within us changes the way we see things. 1 Corinthians 2:12-14 (NLT) says: "We have received God's Spirit (not the world's spirit), so we can know the wonderful things God has freely given us. When we tell you these things, we do not use words that come from human wisdom. Instead, we speak words given to us by the Spirit, using the Spirit's words to explain spiritual truths. But people who aren't spiritual can't receive these truths from God's Spirit. It all sounds foolish to them and they can't understand it, for only those who are spiritual can understand what the Spirit means."

These are a few basic ways you can check that you belong to Jesus and that you know Him. When it comes to spiritual gifts, we still must test the spirits. God has allowed some persons the ability to foretell the future just to test you, too. But the fruits of the Spirit cannot be counterfeited. There will be people who can fake it for a while on the surface, of course. But there are permanent characteristics of the person who truly belongs to Jesus Christ and follows him as Lord. The apostle John wrote the entire letter of 1 John to tell us what they are:

1. We obey Jesus' commands; (1 John 2:3-6)

2. We love our brother; (1 John 2:9-10)

3. We don't love this world or its possessions; (1 John 2:15-17)

4. We don't lead a sinful lifestyle; (1 John 3:9-10)

5. We have compassion in our actions; (1 John 3:16-20)

6. We have the Holy Spirit in us. (1 John 4:13-15)

These assurances are important, because some Christians adamantly believe that psychic or mediumship abilities are not of God, and will still do everything in their power to convince you that as long as you have those abilities, you don't belong to Jesus. In their way of thinking, any psychic or medium who becomes a follower of Jesus Christ couldn't retain these abilities, because the source of the ability (Satan or a demonic spirit, as they see it), would be cast out.

If your abilities were the result of disobeying God and becoming involved in a practice that He has forbidden, then you can be certain the spirit would not be of God, and would have no place in your life with Christ.

The mediums and psychics I know personally, who have always had their psychic or mediumship abilities, did not lose their abilities by becoming a follower of Jesus Christ. Tami, my first girlfriend, continues to be able to make accurate predictions. Melanie serves the Lord Jesus Christ and is still a medium. My wife Stanna serves the Lord with all of her heart, and still has her psychic abilities. And so does my son Ryan.

If your gift or ability was *not* from the Lord, it would *not* benefit your life to continue having it. Any ability resulting from practices that the Lord has said to not do would be inferior to a genuine spiritual gift from the Lord.

Consider too, that an ability derived from a forbidden practice may not necessarily be what the Holy Spirit would determine as being the best choice of a gift for you to have to serve the Lord. Even though I have a book here in my library on how to develop psychic ability, I prefer the gift that the Holy Spirit gave me: Teaching.

That is what he determined was best for me with which to be able to serve Christ — not for me to be psychically gifted. He gave me a wife with that gift, but decided I should be gifted to teach instead.

Romans 11:29 (NLT) says: "God's gifts and his call can never be withdrawn." Once the Holy Spirit gives you a gift, he does not change his mind and take that gift or ability away. The gift may become dormant through not being used, which is why Paul told Timothy to "stir up the gift of God, which is in thee." (2 Timothy 1:6, KJV) He may give you more spiritual gifts in the future (see 1 Corinthians 14:1), but God will never take away any gift He gave you.

What happens to our gifts, though, once we are in the Kingdom of Heaven? Will we still serve the Lord with them? Will we have different gifts?

FIFTEEN
Beyond the Other Side

Our reputation should not rest upon our gifts, but rather what we did with them in this life. At this time, stop and ask yourself: *Do I use my gift to bring glory to Christ Jesus and point others toward him? Do I use my gift as a demonstration of the Spirits' ability while proclaiming to others the way to have eternal life? Do I use my gift to build up others' knowledge, provide them with comfort, help them mature in Christ, bring unity among believers, and do my part in serving followers of Jesus?*

If you use your gift just to amaze others with what you can see and know that they can't, then what have you really accomplished with it? You may have gotten them to believe in the supernatural, but then if they don't take that belief any further, how have you benefitted their lives? While it's true that my amazement with Tami's abilities led to me re-examining my beliefs, and eventually to writing this book, can you be certain that this will be what happens to the people *you* amaze?

Our present spiritual gifts will someday pass. They will not pass in this lifetime, nor in this world, but will at a time in the future beyond all of that. So who we are when we are in the Lord's kingdom will not be connected to the gifts we have now. We won't be calling ourselves by the terms "psychic," medium," "healer," or even "teacher," in that kingdom. Spiritual gifts, even psychic and medium abilities, are merely tools with which to accomplish your work. You are to use your gifts to accomplish the building up of the Kingdom of Heaven, of which you are a citizen. (See Philippians 3:20)

"Love never fails," the Bible says. "But if there are gifts of prophecy, they will be done away; if there are tongues, they will cease; if there is knowledge, it will be done away. For we know in part and we prophesy in part; but when the perfect comes, the partial will be done away." (1 Corinthians 13:8-10, NASB)

What is meant by "when the perfect comes, the partial will be done away?" I once heard it said in a Bible study that "when the perfect comes" meant the time when the Bible would be complete, and "the partial" meant the spiritual gifts. The flaw in this kind of thinking is this: If spiritual gifts were meant to be taken away by God upon completion of the Scriptures, you would then have an *imperfect* Bible — because, then, all teachings in the Bible regarding the gifts of the Spirit would be out of date.

Jesus said, "You will receive power when the Holy Spirit has come upon you," (Acts 1:8, NASB), and "Heaven and earth shall pass away: but my words shall not pass away." (Mark 13:31, KJV) These two Scriptures, when taken together, assure us that when Jesus says we will receive the power of the Holy Spirit, that truth is *never* going to ever be obsolete or outdated! The Spirit will continue to empower us. It doesn't take a great knowledge of the Bible for us to know that this world is not perfect, anyway. So as long as we serve Christ in an imperfect world, there will be spiritual gifts with which to do our work.

The Bible continues: "Now we see things imperfectly, like puzzling reflections in a mirror, but then we will see everything with perfect clarity. All that I know now is partial and incomplete, but then I will know everything completely, just as God now knows me completely. Three things will last forever — faith, hope, and love — and the greatest of these is love." (1 Corinthians 13:12-13, NLT)

This means that in the future, i.e., at the time "the perfect" comes, we will "know everything completely." We will get the answers to the questions that we don't know now, or only have theories about what the answer should be.

But when is this perfection supposed to occur? The 21st chapter of Revelation tells about the New Jerusalem coming down out of Heaven, and the 27th verse of the chapter is describing perfection when it says: "Nothing evil will be allowed to enter, nor anyone who practices shameful idolatry and dishonesty — but only those whose names are written in the Lamb's Book of Life." (Revelation 21:27, NLT)

This is *after* the new Heaven and new Earth have been created, after the old Heaven and Earth have passed away, because that is what it says in Revelation 21:1. The city *came down* from Heaven to the new Earth. Another way we know perfection comes then is because this is *after* Death and Hades, and anyone not in the Book of Life, was thrown into the lake of fire. (See Revelation 20:13-15)

At that time we will no longer have need for faith and hope, because our hopes will have been fulfilled, and the faith needed for believing in that hope has reached its realization. So the greatest of them all — love — shall remain.

We will have a different body — a supernatural, glorified body — when we are in the Kingdom of Heaven. Paul talks about this body in 1 Corinthians 15:42-44 (NASB), but only uses comparisons to describe just how different this body is from the one we have now: "It is sown a perishable body, it is raised an imperishable body; it is sown in dishonor, it is raised in glory; it is sown in weakness, it is raised in power; it is sown a natural body, it is raised a spiritual body. If there is a natural body, there is also a spiritual body."

If we get new bodies, will we recognize each other? I believe that we will, but it will be when the Spirit brings that recognition to our minds. When Jesus first rose from the dead, Mary Magdalene didn't recognize him at first. The Bible says in John 20:14-18, that she turned around and saw Jesus standing there, but did not realize that it was Jesus. Thinking he was the gardener, she asked where Jesus' body had been put. But as he called her name, she instantly recognized him.

There is a very similar story about Jesus appearing to two of his followers who were on the road walking from Jerusalem to Emmaus in Luke 24:13-34. This was a seven-mile walk, and Jesus was talking with these two all the way to their destination. They urged him to stay at their house, and the Bible says: "As they sat down to eat, he took the bread and blessed it. Then he broke it and gave it to them. Suddenly, their eyes were opened, and they recognized him. And at that moment he disappeared!" (Luke 24:30-31, NLT)

Luke 24:31 gives us one example of the kind of powers this supernatural body has — to simply disappear. Another is given in John 20:19 (HCSB): "In the evening of that first day of the week, the disciples were gathered together with the doors locked because of their fear of the Jews. Then Jesus came, stood among them, and said to them, 'Peace to you!'" And he gave an encore demonstration of that power — to be able to appear in a room, even with the doors locked — just one week later, because the Bible tells us: "After eight days His disciples were indoors again, and Thomas was with them. Even though the doors were locked, Jesus came and stood among them. He said, 'Peace to you!'" (John 20:26, HCSB)

This was with a solid, touchable body. The idea that this was a ghost or spirit was already in the disciples' mind the first time, because we read: "The whole group was startled and frightened, thinking they were seeing a ghost! 'Why are you frightened?' he asked. 'Why are your hearts filled with doubt? Look at my hands. Look at my feet. You can see that it's really me. Touch me and make sure that I am not a ghost, because ghosts don't have bodies, as you see that I do.' As he spoke, he showed them his hands and his feet. Still they stood there in disbelief, filled with joy and wonder. Then he asked them, 'Do you have anything here to eat?' They gave him a piece of broiled fish, and he ate it as they watched." (Luke 24:37-43, NLT)

It was so important to Jesus that his followers know that he actually rose from the dead and had a body, that he not only invited them to touch him, but he ate food in front of them, too. Don't forget that there were mediums and other people who had seen spirits in those times as well. To appear to the disciples as a spirit would mean nothing to them. But to rise from the dead with an actual body proved he conquered death and was the Son of God.

We will also be taking part in judging in Heaven. Paul said, in 1 Corinthians 6:2-3 (KJV): "Do ye not know that the saints shall judge the world? And if the world shall be judged by you, are ye unworthy to judge the smallest matters? Know ye not that we shall judge angels?" Note something in Paul's wording here — "saint" means *you!* By first saying "the saints shall judge the world," followed by "the world shall be judged by you," Paul directly implies that a "saint" is *any* follower of Jesus — not a person approved by the Catholic Church.

This is not the judgment of *people.* As you have already read, we will all go through that judgment ourselves. This is a judgment of *things* and of *angels.* "He that is spiritual judgeth all things, yet he himself is judged of no man." (1 Corinthians 2:15, KJV) Angels are powerful beings, but they speak of themselves as servants of the Lord just like you and I. In the very last chapter of the Bible,

Revelation 22, the apostle John writes: "I fell down to worship at the feet of the angel. . .but he said, "No, don't worship me. I am a servant of God, just like you and your brothers the prophets, as well as all who obey what is written in this book. Worship only God!" (Revelation 22:8-9, NLT)

If this is true — that angels serve God like you and I — then why do so many books emphasize calling upon the angels, and communicating with the angels so much, if they are just servants of the Lord like you and I? Is it perhaps to take the focus off of Jesus Christ? Colossians 2:18-19 (NLT) warns us: "Don't let anyone condemn you by insisting on pious self-denial or the worship of angels, saying they have had visions about these things. Their sinful minds have made them proud, and they are not connected to Christ, the head of the body. For he holds the whole body together with its joints and ligaments, and it grows as God nourishes it."

Note from these verses that when you lose connection with Jesus, your mind is *sinful*. You cannot grow spiritually without Jesus. He is *the* Son of God, *the* only way to the Father, *the* one who created all things, and the one who is *greater* than all of the angels.

Yes, Jesus is *greater* than all of the angels. The Bible says in Hebrews 1:3-4 (NLT): "The Son radiates God's own glory and expresses the very character of God, and he sustains everything by the mighty power of his command. When he had cleansed us from our sins, he sat down in the place of honor at the right hand of the majestic God in heaven. This shows that the Son is far greater than the angels, just as the name God gave him is greater than their names."

That same chapter tells us more about angels: "Angels are only servants — spirits sent to care for people who will inherit salvation." (Hebrews 1:14, NLT) You serve Christ. Angels serve you.

Have you ever seen an angel? You probably have and didn't know it. Hebrews 13:2 tells us in the *New Living Translation:* "Don't forget to show hospitality to strangers, for some who have done this have entertained angels without realizing it!"

Jesus hasn't forgotten about our rewards, either. I have mentioned in past chapters about working for the Lord and serving Him, to prepare you for this time in the Kingdom of Heaven. Jesus says in Revelation 22:12-13 (NLT): "I am coming soon, bringing my reward with me to repay all people according to their deeds. I am the Alpha and the Omega, the First and the Last, the Beginning and the End."

Not only will we have the rewards, and the treasure we have laid up in Heaven, but we will be given possessions of our own. And we will have work to do in Heaven, too. Revelation 22:3 (KJV) tells us: "The throne of God and of the Lamb shall be in it; *and his servants shall serve him.*" So if the present spiritual gifts have passed, will we have new spiritual gifts to carry out our new work? If even an earthly employer furnishes us with what we need to do our jobs, and the Holy Spirit furnished us with spiritual power to work for the Lord in this world, would it not seem likely that the Lord will again furnish spiritual power for us to accomplish our work in the Kingdom of Heaven?

Paul wrote: "All that I know now is partial and incomplete, but then I will know everything completely." (1 Corinthians 13:12, NLT) It would logically follow that if we would "know everything completely," these new spiritual tools will not be psychic or mediumship abilities. Since both of these spiritual gifts are means to supernaturally gain knowledge, they will have been made obsolete in the Kingdom of Heaven — in much the same way as a dial telephone, answering machine, typewriter, or record player are now obsolete in this world — because there would be no further knowledge to gain or progress to be made by the use of these gifts.

We won't be married in Heaven, because Jesus said: "For when the dead rise, they will neither marry nor be given in marriage. In this respect they will be like the angels in heaven." (Matthew 22:30, NLT)

We will have friends in Heaven, though, for Luke 16:9 (NLT) says: "Use your worldly resources to benefit others and make friends. Then, when your earthly possessions are gone, they will welcome you to an eternal home." This verse seems to say that the friends we make here — the ones that serve the Lord — will also be there to "welcome us to an eternal home."

What about our friends and others who *don't* serve the Lord? What if we go through Heaven, and can't find someone we cared a lot for, and find they never made it? Won't we be sad to know that?

That's not going to happen. The Bible tells us in Isaiah 65:17 (NASB): "Behold, I create new heavens and a new earth; and the former things will not be remembered or come to mind." This is both a blessing and a punishment. It is a blessing to those who are with Jesus, because they won't be able to even remember anyone who never made it.

This also extends to the possessions we have, and the fun things we did with them on Earth. We won't miss the stuff we left behind because we will not be able to remember our houses, cars, computers, iPods, cell phones, or anything else.

The punishment is for those who are in the fire that is never quenched, where they are in torment, and there is weeping and gnashing of teeth. Add this to all of those punishments: They will be able to see Heaven from far off, and see that *no one remembers them at all.* No one misses them. No one even cares what happened to them, *because* no one can remember them. All they have is an eternity of torment, fire, weeping and gnashing of teeth.

You can call it Hell, or you can even pretend that it doesn't exist. You will have all eternity to ask yourself why you didn't accept a very generous gift of salvation from a God who loved you so much he didn't want to send you there, and shed the blood of his only Son so you wouldn't have had to go.

But the 18th and 19th verses of Isaiah 65 (NASB) say: "Be glad and rejoice forever in what I create; for behold, I create Jerusalem for rejoicing, and her people for gladness. I will also rejoice in Jerusalem and be glad in My people; and there will no longer be heard in her the voice of weeping and the sound of crying."

Disneyland is sometimes referred to as "the happiest place on earth." Can you imagine living in "the happiest place in the Kingdom of Heaven?" Everything we have read so far about the Kingdom of Heaven is far superior to whatever is in this world; the New Jerusalem would have to be a place hundreds of times better than Disneyland — *and without the admission price.* Isaiah 55:1-2 (HCSB) says: "Come, everyone who is thirsty, come to the waters; and you without money, come, buy, and eat! Come, buy wine and milk, without money and without cost! Why do you spend money on what is not food, and your wages on what does not satisfy?"

And Revelation 22:17 (NLT) also says: "The Spirit and the bride say, 'Come.' Let anyone who hears this say, 'Come.' Let anyone who is thirsty come. Let anyone who desires drink freely from the water of life."

This, then — the Kingdom of Heaven, and not merely "the other side"— is your final destination. Don't even simply think of harps, halos, and golden streets, because the Bible says: "No eye has seen, no ear has heard, and no mind has imagined what God has prepared for those who love him." (1 Corinthians 2:8-10, NLT) We know, however, that the Bible promises that the Kingdom of Heaven will be a place of delight and joy — *unimaginable joy!*

Your spiritual gifts are given to you by the Spirit of the Lord for you to have your part in making the Kingdom of Heaven the final destination for as many persons as possible. May the Lord reward you greatly when you stand before Him and say, "Lord, thank you for the spiritual gifts you entrusted to me. Thank you for letting my gifts show the world that you are an amazing, loving God, with purpose for each of our lives. You entrusted me with these gifts, and now, Lord, here are the people whose lives I have touched and led to you with my gifts so that they may have a future with you forever in your kingdom."

BIBLIOGRAPHY

Hobbs, Herschel H (1971). *The Baptist Faith and Message.* Nashville, TN: Convention Press.

The Holy Bible, Holman Christian Standard Bible. Nashville, TN: 2003, Holman Bible Publishers.

The Holy Bible, New American Standard Version. La Habra, CA: The Lockman Foundation, 1995

The Holy Bible, New International Version. Grand Rapids, MI: 1985, Zondervan Bible Publishers.

The Holy Bible, New Living Translation. Carol Stream, Illinois: 1996, 2004, 2007, Tyndale House Publishers, Inc.,

McDowell, J. (1972) *Evidence Which Demands A Verdict.* San Bernardino, CA: Campus Crusade for Christ International.

Parapsychology Review. Published bimonthly from 1970 to 1990 by the Parapsychology Foundation, Inc. New York, NY.

Pink, A. W. (1917) *The Divine Inspiration of the Bible.* Retrieved from: http://www.ccel.org/ccel/pink/inspiration.txt

Scofield, C. I. (Ed.). (1917). *The Scofield Reference Bible.* New York: Oxford University Press, American Branch.

Urquhart, J. (1895). *The Inspiration and Accuracy of the Holy Scriptures.* Retrieved from:
http://archive.org/stream/theinspirationac00urquuoft#page/n5/mode/2up.

REFERENCES

"Familiar" (1828). In Webster's Revised Unabridged Dictionary (1913 + 1828). Retrieved from: http://machaut.uchicago.edu/websters.

General Council of the Assemblies of God (2010). *Assemblies of God Fundamental Truths*. Retrieved from: http://ag.org/top/Beliefs/Statement_of_fundamental_truths/sft_shor t.cfm.

"Lord" (1828). In Webster's Revised Unabridged Dictionary (1913 + 1828). Retrieved from http://machaut.uchicago.edu/websters.

"Spiritist" (1913). In Webster's Revised Unabridged Dictionary (1913 + 1828). Retrieved from: http://machaut.uchicago.edu/websters.

"Spiritualist" (1913). In Webster's Revised Unabridged Dictionary (1913 + 1828). Retrieved from: http://machaut.uchicago.edu/websters.

"Wizard" (1828, 1913). In *Webster's Revised Unabridged Dictionary (1913 + 1828)*. Retrieved from: http://machaut.uchicago.edu/websters.

AUTHOR'S NOTES

I acknowledge the divinity of Jesus Christ. To make easier reading for the reader, however, we have chosen not to capitalize the "H" when referring to God or Jesus as in "Him" or "He."

ABOUT THE AUTHOR

Kevin Schoeppel's interest in psychics began in 1975 when he fell in love with a girl who could predict the future. This relationship sparked his interest in social attitudes toward psychics, as well as in discovering whatever he could about how psychic ability worked. He married his wife, Stanna — a psychic — in 1978.

Kevin was raised in Southern Baptist churches, and began teaching the Bible in 1992. In 1999 he was ordained as a deacon by Pima Street Baptist Church of Tucson, and in 2006 was elected adult education director of the church. While teaching Bible classes in the mid-2000s, his students began having more questions for Kevin on what the Bible really says about spirits, psychics, and mediums. At the same time, he began to make friends with psychics and mediums through online social networking, many of whom were pleasantly surprised at his unconditional acceptance of them. Kevin lives near Tucson, Arizona, with Stanna and their son Ryan.

Kevin is available for speaking engagements and interviews. Contact Kevin by email: KevinSchoeppel@yahoo.com. Website: www.BibleForPsychics.com.

Photo credit: Ryan Schoeppel

CPSIA information can be obtained
at www.ICGtesting.com
Printed in the USA
LVHW062154051021
699629LV00024B/477